Northeast Community Tree Guide:
Benefits, Costs, and Strategic Planting

by E. Gregory McPherson, James R. Simpson, Paula J. Peper,
Shelley L. Gardner, Kelaine E. Vargas, and Qingfu Xiao

U.S. Department of Agriculture, Forest Service
Pacific Southwest Research Station
Albany, CA
August 2007

Contributing Organizations
USDA Forest Service
Pacific Southwest Research Station
Center for Urban Forest Research
Davis, CA

Department of Land, Air, and Water Resources
University of California
Davis, CA

Sponsoring Organizations
USDA Forest Service
State and Private Forestry
Urban and Community Forestry Program

Abstract

McPherson, E. Gregory; Simpson, James R.; Peper, Paula J.; Gardner, Shelley L.; Vargas, Kelaine E.; Xiao, Qingfu. 2007. Northeast community tree guide: benefits, costs, and strategic planting. Gen. Tech. Rep. PSW-GTR-202. Albany, CA: U.S. Department of Agriculture, Forest Service, Pacific Southwest Research Station. 106 p.

Trees make our cities more attractive and provide many ecosystem services, including air quality improvement, energy conservation, stormwater interception, and atmospheric carbon dioxide reduction. These benefits must be weighed against the costs of maintaining trees, including planting, pruning, irrigation, administration, pest control, liability, cleanup, and removal. We present benefits and costs for representative small, medium, and large deciduous trees and coniferous trees in the Northeast region derived from models based on indepth research carried out in the borough of Queens, New York City. Average annual net benefits (benefits minus costs) increase with mature tree size and differ based on location: $5 (yard) to $9 (public) for a small tree, $36 (yard) to $52 (public) for a medium tree, $85 (yard) to $113 (public) for a large tree, $21 (yard) to $33 (public) for a conifer. Two hypothetical examples of planting projects are described to illustrate how the data in this guide can be adapted to local uses, and guidelines for maximizing benefits and reducing costs are given.

Keywords: Ecosystem services, Northeast, urban forestry, benefit-cost analysis.

What's in This Tree Guide?

This tree guide is organized as follows:

Executive Summary: Presents key findings.

Chapter 1: Describes the guide's purpose, audience, and geographic scope.

Chapter 2: Provides background information on the potential of trees in Northeast communities to provide benefits and describes management costs that are typically incurred.

Chapter 3: Provides calculations of tree benefits and costs for the Northeast region.

Chapter 4: Illustrates how to estimate urban forest benefits and costs for tree planting projects in your community and tips to increase cost-effectiveness.

Chapter 5: Presents guidelines for selecting and placing trees in residential yards and public open spaces.

Appendix 1: Recommends additional resources for further information.

Appendix 2: Contains tables that list annual benefits and costs of representative tree species at 5-year intervals for 40 years after planting.

Appendix 3: Describes the methods, assumptions, and limitations associated with estimating tree benefits and costs.

Glossary of terms: Provides definitions for technical terms used in the report.

References: Lists references cited in the guide.

This guide will help users quantify the long-term benefits and costs associated with proposed tree planting projects. It is available online at http://cufr.ucdavis.edu/products.

The Center for Urban Forest Research (CUFR) has developed a computer program called STRATUM to estimate these values for existing street and park trees. STRATUM is part of the i-Tree software suite. More information on i-Tree and STRATUM is available at www.itreetools.org and the CUFR Web site.

The green infrastructure is a significant component of communities in the Northeast region.

Executive Summary

This report quantifies benefits and costs for small, medium, and large deciduous trees and one coniferous tree in the Northeast region: the species chosen as representative are Kwanzan cherry, red maple, Japanese zelkova, and eastern white pine, respectively (see "Common and Scientific Names" section). The analysis describes "yard" trees (those planted in residential sites) and "public trees" (those planted on streets or in parks). We assume a 66 percent survival rate over a 40-year timeframe. Tree care costs and mortality rates are based on results from a survey of municipal and commercial arborists. Benefits are calculated by using tree growth curves and numerical models that consider regional climate, building characteristics, air pollutant concentrations, and prices.

The measurements used in modeling environmental and other benefits of trees are based on indepth research carried out in the Borough of Queens, New York City. Given the Northeast region's large and diverse geographical area, this approach provides first-order approximations. It is a general accounting that can be easily adapted and adjusted for local planting projects. Two examples are provided that illustrate how to adjust benefits and costs to reflect different aspects of local planting projects.

Large trees provide the most benefits. Average annual benefits increase with mature tree size:

- $26 to $30 for a small tree

- $69 to $79 for a medium tree

- $125 to $147 for a large tree

- $54 to $56 for a conifer

Benefits associated with energy savings and increased property value account for the largest proportion of total benefits in this region. Reduced stormwater runoff, lower levels of air pollutants, and less carbon dioxide in the air are the next most important benefits.

Energy conservation benefits differ with tree location as well as size. Trees located opposite west-facing walls provide the greatest net heating and cooling energy savings. Reducing heating and cooling energy needs reduces carbon dioxide emissions and thereby reduces atmospheric carbon dioxide. Similarly, energy savings that reduce pollutant emissions at power plants account for important reductions in gases that produce ozone, a major component of smog.

The average annual costs for tree care range from $20 to $40 per tree.

- $22 (yard) and $20 (public) for a small tree

- $33 (yard) and $27 (public) for a medium tree

Benefits and costs quantified

Average annual benefits

Costs

- $40 (yard) and $34 (public) for a large tree

- $33 (yard) and $23 (public) for a conifer

Planting is the greatest cost for trees (annualized to $10 to $15 per tree per year). Tree pruning is the next highest expense ($4 to $18 per tree per year). Tree care expenditures tend to increase with mature tree size because of increased labor and equipment costs.

Average annual net benefits

Average annual net benefits (benefits minus costs) per tree for a 40-year period are as follows:

- $5 (yard) to $9 (public) for a small tree

- $36 (yard) to $52 (public) for a medium tree

- $85 (yard) to $113 (public) for a large tree

- $21 (yard) to $33 (public) for a conifer

Environmental benefits alone, including energy savings, stormwater-runoff reduction, improved air quality, and reduced atmospheric carbon dioxide, are up to four times tree care costs.

Net benefits summed over 40 years

Net benefits for a yard tree opposite a west wall and a public tree are substantial when summed over the entire 40-year period:

- $320 (yard) and $364 (public) for a small tree

- $1,849 (yard) and $2,066 (public) for a medium tree

- $4,261 (yard) and $4,531 (public) for a large tree

- $855 (yard) and $1,322 (public) for a conifer

Public trees produce higher net benefits than private trees. Our survey results indicate that this is primarily due to lower maintenance costs for street and park trees. The standard of care is often lower for public trees because municipal budgets tend to reflect what is allocated, not what is needed to maintain a healthy urban forest.

To demonstrate how communities can adapt the information in this report to their needs, the benefits and costs of different planting projects are determined for two fictional cities interested in increasing their urban forest. In the hypothetical city of Rodbell Falls, net benefits and benefit-cost ratios (BCRs) are calculated for a planting of 1,000 trees (2-in caliper) assuming a cost of $300 per tree, 66 percent survival rate, and 40-year analysis. Total costs are $970,484, benefits total $4.6 million, and net benefits are $3.6 million ($90 per tree per year). The BCR is 4.69:1, indicating that $4.69 is returned for every $1 invested. The net benefits and BCRs by mature tree size are:

- $21,466 (1.67:1) for 50 small flowering Kwanzan cherry trees
- $314,641 (3.47:1) for 150 medium red maple trees
- $3.1 million (5.25:1) for 700 large Japanese zelkova trees
- $128,093 (2.64:1) for 100 eastern white pine trees

Increased property values (44 percent) and reduced energy costs (34 percent) account for more than three-quarters of the estimated benefits. Reduced storm-water runoff (11 percent), improved air quality (9 percent), and atmospheric carbon dioxide reduction (1 percent) make up the remaining benefits.

In the fictional city of Buscainoville, long-term planting and tree care costs and benefits were compared to determine if a proposed policy that favors planting small trees would be cost-effective compared to the current policy of planting large trees where space permits. Over a 40-year period, the net benefits would be:

- $262 per tree for a Kwanzan cherry
- $1,923 per tree for a red maple
- $4,321 per tree for a Japanese zelkova

Based on this analysis, the city of Buscainoville decided to retain their policy. They now require tree shade plans that show how developers will achieve 50 percent shade over streets, sidewalks, and parking lots within 15 years of development.

Contents

Trees grace a residential street in New York City.

Chapter 1. Introduction

The Northeast Region

From small towns surrounded by cropland, forests, and the sea, to the city of New York, the Nation's largest city, the Northeast region (fig. 1) contains a diverse assemblage of communities. The Northeast region is home to approximately 25 million people. The region extends southwest along a narrow band bordering Lake Ontario in New York and touches the tip of Ohio near Lake Erie before turning east across much of Pennsylvania and finally sweeping north along the Atlantic Coast through Connecticut, Massachusetts, New Hampshire, and ending along the lower tip of coastal Maine. The region also includes small portions of Virginia, West Virginia, Maryland, and New Jersey (fig. 1). Boundaries correspond with Sunset Climate Zones 34, 37 through 40, and 42 (Brenzel 2001) and USDA Hardiness Zones 5 through 7. The Great Lakes and Atlantic Ocean influence the **climate**[1] in this region, allowing a greater number of tree species to thrive than in regions farther north and inland. There is a strong annual temperature cycle, with cold winters and warm summers. Average annual temperatures range from 40 to 65 °F. The New England interior and lowland Maine are the coldest areas within the region with the shortest growing season. Normal lows here can range from -2 to 18 °F. However, regular rainfall

Geographic scope of the Northeast region

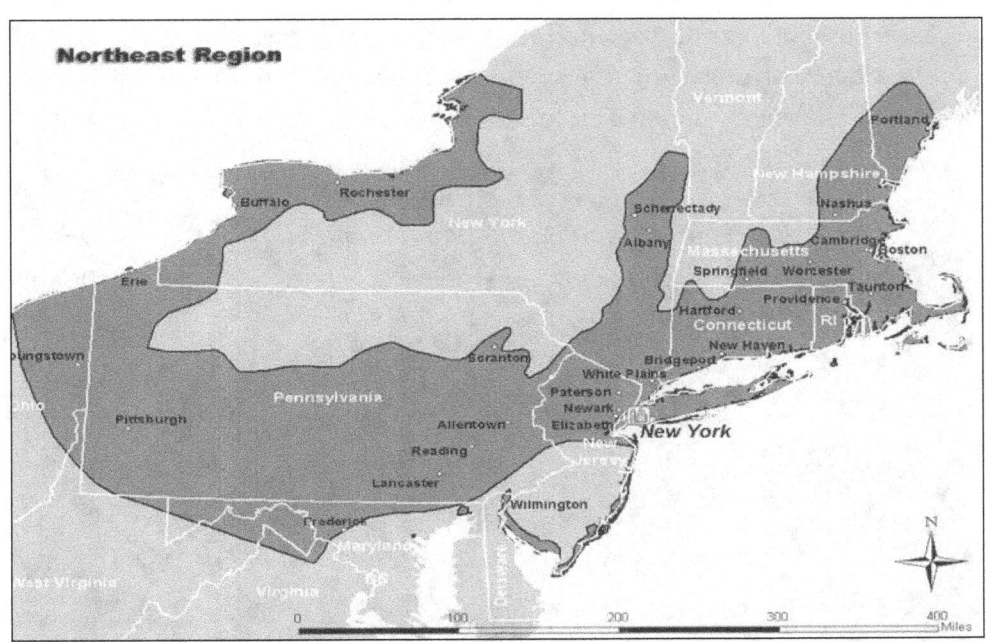

Figure 1—The Northeast region (shaded area) extends southwest along a narrow band bordering Lake Ontario in New York and touches the tip of Ohio near Lake Erie before turning east across much of Pennsylvania and finally sweeping north along the Atlantic Coast through Connecticut, Massachusetts, New Hampshire, and ending along the lower tip of coastal Maine. The region also includes small portions of Virginia, West Virginia, Maryland, and New Jersey.

[1] Words in bold are defined in the glossary.

combined with excellent soils provide gardeners with the opportunity to plant a wide range of tree, shrub, and flower species. Annual precipitation throughout the Northeast ranges from 30 to 50 in annually.

In the Northeast region, urban forest canopies form living umbrellas. They are distinctive features of the landscape that protect us from the elements, clean the water we drink and the air we breathe, and form a living connection to earlier generations who planted and tended these trees.

Northeast communities can derive many benefits from community forests

As the communities of the Northeast continue to grow during the coming decades, sustaining healthy **community forests** is integral to the quality of life residents experience. The role of urban forests in enhancing the environment, increasing community attractiveness and livability, and fostering civic pride takes on greater significance as communities strive to balance economic growth with environmental quality and social well-being. The simple act of planting trees provides opportunities to connect residents with nature and with each other. Neighborhood tree plantings and stewardship projects stimulate investment by local citizens, businesses, and governments for the betterment of their communities (fig. 2). Community forests bring opportunity for economic renewal, combating development woes, improving human health, and increasing the quality of life for community residents.

Quality of life improves with trees

Northeast communities can promote energy efficiency through tree planting and stewardship programs that strategically locate trees to save energy and minimize conflicts with urban infrastructure. The same trees can provide additional benefits by reducing stormwater runoff; improving local air, soil, and water quality;

Figure 2—Tree planting and stewardship programs provide opportunities for local residents to work together to build better communities.

reducing atmospheric carbon dioxide; providing wildlife habitat; increasing property values; slowing traffic; enhancing community attractiveness and investment; and promoting human health and well-being.

This guide builds upon previous studies by the USDA Forest Service in Brooklyn (Nowak et al. 2002), Chicago and Sacramento (McPherson 1998, McPherson et al. 1997), American Forest's urban ecosystem analyses in Washington D.C. (American Forests 2002) and Detroit (American Forests 2006), and tree guides for the Midwest and Piedmont regions (McPherson et al. 2006a, and 2006b) to extend existing knowledge of urban forest benefits in the Northeast. The guide:

Scope defined

- Quantifies benefits of trees on a per-tree basis rather than on a canopy-cover basis (it should not be used to estimate benefits for trees growing in forest stands).

- Describes management costs and benefits.

- Details benefits and costs for trees in residential yards and along streets and in parks.

- Illustrates how to use this information to estimate benefits and costs for local tree planting projects.

These guidelines are specific to the Northeast and are based on measurements and calculations from open-growing urban trees in this region.

Street, park, and shade trees are components of all Northeast communities, and they impact every resident. Their benefits are myriad. However, with municipal tree programs dependent on taxpayer-supported general funds, communities are forced to ask whether trees are worth the price to plant and care for over the long term, thus requiring urban forestry programs to demonstrate their cost-effectiveness (McPherson 1995). If tree plantings are proven to benefit communities, then monetary commitment to tree programs will be justified. Therefore, the objective of this tree guide is to identify and describe the benefits and costs of planting trees in Northeast communities—providing a tool for municipal tree managers, arborists, and tree enthusiasts to increase public awareness and support for trees (Dwyer and Miller 1999).

Audience and objectives

This tree guide addresses a number of questions about the environmental and aesthetic benefits of community tree plantings in Northeast communities:

What will this tree guide do?

- How can tree-planting programs improve environmental quality, conserve energy, and add value to communities?

- Where should residential yard and public trees be placed to maximize their benefits and cost-effectiveness?

- How can conflicts between trees and power lines, sidewalks, and buildings be minimized?

3

Trees in Northeast communities enhance quality of life (photo courtesy of Phillip Rodbell).

Chapter 2. Identifying Benefits and Costs of Urban and Community Forests

This chapter describes benefits and costs of public and privately managed trees. Benefits and associated economic value of community forests are described. Expenditures related to tree care and management are assessed—a necessary process for creating cost-effective programs (Dwyer et al. 1992, Hudson 1983).

Benefits

Saving Energy

Energy is an essential ingredient for quality of life and for economic growth. Conserving energy by greening our cities is often more cost-effective than building new power plants. For example, while California was experiencing energy shortages in 2001, its 177 million city trees were providing shade and conserving energy. Annual savings to utilities was an estimated $500 million in wholesale electricity and generation purchases (McPherson and Simpson 2003). Planting 50 million more shade trees in strategic locations would provide savings equivalent to seven 100-megawatt power plants. The cost of peak load reduction was $63/kW, considerably less than the $150/kW amount that is deemed cost-effective. Like electric utilities throughout the country, utilities in the Northeast could invest in shade tree programs as a cost-effective energy conservation measure.

How trees work to save energy

Trees modify climate and conserve building energy use in three principal ways (fig. 3):

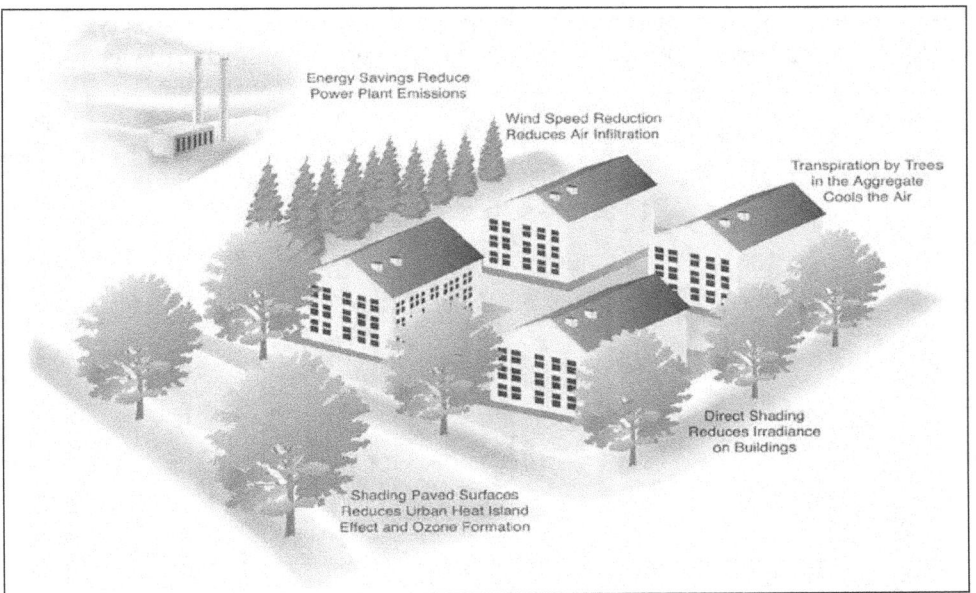

Figure 3—Trees save energy for heating and cooling by shading buildings, lowering summertime temperatures, and reducing windspeeds. Secondary benefits from energy conservation are reduced water consumption and reduced pollutant emissions by power plants (drawing by Mike Thomas).

- Shading reduces the amount of heat absorbed and stored by built surfaces.

- **Evapotranspiration** converts liquid water to water vapor and thus cools the air by using solar energy that would otherwise result in heating of the air.

- Windspeed reduction reduces the infiltration of outside air into interior spaces and reduces heat loss, especially where conductivity is relatively high (e.g., glass windows) (Simpson 1998).

Trees lower temperatures

Trees and other vegetation on individual building sites may lower air temperatures 5 °F compared with outside the **greenspace**. At larger scales (6 mi²), temperature differences of more than 9 °F have been observed between city centers and more vegetated suburban areas (Akbari et al. 1992). These "hot spots" in cities are called **urban heat island**s. A recent study for New York City compared trees, living roofs, and light surfaces and found that curbside tree planting was the most effective heat island mitigation strategy (Rosenzweig et al. 2006).

Trees increase home energy efficiency and save money

For individual buildings, strategically placed trees can increase energy efficiency in the summer and winter. Because the summer sun is low in the east and west for several hours each day, solar angles should be considered. Trees that shade east and, especially, west walls help keep buildings cool (fig. 4). In the winter, allowing the sun to strike the southern side of a building can warm interior spaces. However, the trunks and bare branches of **deciduous** trees that shade south- and east-facing walls during winter may increase heating costs by blocking 40 percent or more of winter irradiance (McPherson 1984).

Windbreaks reduce heat loss

Rates at which outside air infiltrates a building can increase substantially with windspeed. In cold, windy weather, the entire volume of air, even in newer or tightly sealed homes, may change every 2 to 3 hours. Windbreaks reduce

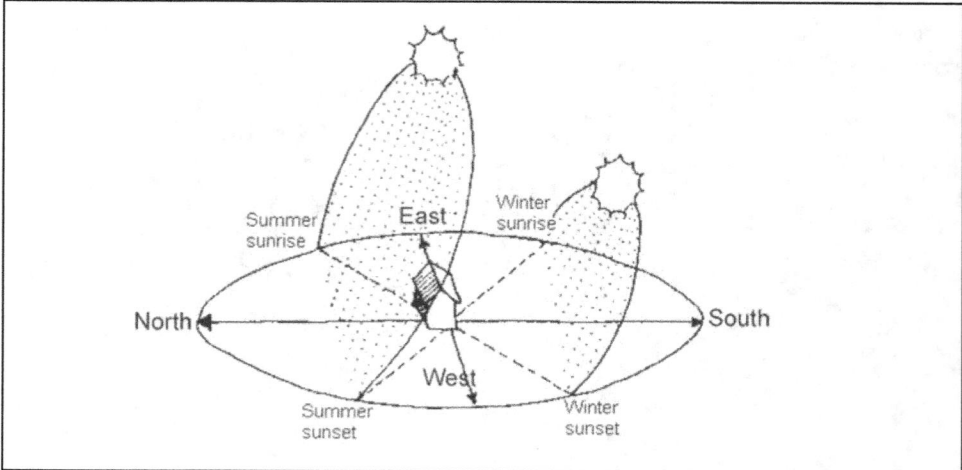

Figure 4—Paths of the sun on winter and summer solstices (from Sand 1991). Summer heat gain is primarily through east- and west-facing windows and walls. The roof receives most irradiance, but insulated attics reduce heat gain to living spaces. The winter sun, at a lower angle, strikes the south-facing surfaces.

windspeed and resulting air infiltration by up to 50 percent, translating into potential annual heating savings of 10 to 12 percent (Heisler 1986). Reductions in windspeed reduce heat transfer through conductive materials as well. Cool winter winds, blowing against windows, can contribute significantly to the heating load of buildings by increasing the gradient between inside and outside temperatures. Windbreaks reduce air infiltration and conductive heat loss from buildings.

Trees provide greater energy savings in the Northeast region than in milder climate regions because they can have greater effects during the cold winters and warm summers. An average energy-efficient home in Boston, Massachusetts, costs about $750 each year for heating and $100 for cooling. A computer simulation demonstrated that three 25-ft tall trees—two on the west side and one on the east side of the house—were estimated to save $25 each year for heating (3 **MBtu**) and $25 for cooling (250 **kWh**), a 6-percent reduction in annual heating and cooling costs (McPherson et al. 1993). Conserving energy by greening our cities is important because it can be more cost-effective than building new power plants (see http://www.fs.fed.us/psw/programs/cufr/products/3/cufr_148.pdf). In the Northeast region, there is ample opportunity to "retrofit" communities with more sustainable landscapes through strategic tree planting and care of existing trees.

Retrofit for more savings

Reducing Atmospheric Carbon Dioxide

Global temperatures have increased since the late 19th century, with major warming periods from 1910 to 1945 and from 1976 to the present (IPCC 2001). Human activities, primarily fossil-fuel consumption, are adding greenhouse gases to the atmosphere, and current research suggests that the recent increases in temperature can be attributed in large part to increases in greenhouse gases (IPCC 2001). Higher global temperatures are expected to have a number of adverse effects, including melting polar ice caps which could raise sea level by 6 to 37 in (Hamburg et al. 1997). With more than one-third of the world's population living in coastal areas (Cohen et al. 1997), the effects could be disastrous. Increasing frequency and duration of extreme weather events will continue to tax emergency management resources. Some plants and animals may become extinct as habitat becomes restricted.

Urban forests have been recognized as important storage sites for carbon dioxide (CO_2), the primary greenhouse gas (Nowak and Crane 2002). At the same time, private markets dedicated to reducing CO_2 emissions by trading carbon credits are emerging (McHale 2003, CO_2e.com 2005). Carbon credits are selling for up to $18 per **ton** ($CO_2$e.com 2005). For every $18 spent on a tree planting project in Arizona, 1 ton of atmospheric CO_2 was reduced (McPherson and Simpson 1999). As carbon

Trees reduce CO_2

Figure 5—Trees sequester carbon dioxide (CO_2) as they grow and indirectly reduce CO_2 emissions from power plants through energy conservation. At the same time, CO_2 is released through decomposition and tree care activities that involve fossil-fuel consumption (drawing by Mike Thomas).

trading markets become accredited and prices rise, these markets could provide monetary resources for community forestry programs.

Urban forests can reduce atmospheric CO_2 in two ways (fig. 5):

- Trees directly sequester CO_2 in their stems and leaves while they grow.

- Trees near buildings can reduce the demand for heating and air conditioning, thereby reducing emissions associated with power production.

Some tree-related activities release CO_2

On the other hand, vehicles, chain saws, chippers, and other equipment release CO_2 during the process of planting and maintaining trees. And eventually, all trees die, and most of the CO_2 that has accumulated in their structure is released into the atmosphere through decomposition. The rate of release into the atmosphere depends on if and how the wood is reused. For instance, recycling of urban wood waste into products such as furniture can delay the rate of decomposition compared to its reuse as mulch.

Avoided CO_2 emissions

Typically, CO_2 released owing to tree planting, maintenance, and other program-related activities is about 2 to 8 percent of annual CO_2 reductions obtained through sequestration and avoided power plant emissions (McPherson and Simpson 1999). To provide a complete picture of atmospheric CO_2 reductions from tree plantings, it is important to consider CO_2 released into the atmosphere through tree planting and care activities, as well as decomposition of wood from pruned or dead trees.

Regional variations in climate and the mix of fuels that produce energy to heat and cool buildings influence potential CO_2 emission reductions. The regional weighted average emission rate is 1,062 lb CO_2/kWh (US EPA 2003). The relatively large amount of coal (29 percent) and oil (10 percent) in the mix of fuels used to generate electricity results in a regional emission rate that is higher than in some other regions. For example, the two-state average for Oregon and Washington is only 308 lb CO_2/kWh, because hydroelectric power predominates. The Northeast region's relatively high CO_2 emission rate means greater benefits from reduced energy demand relative to other regions with lower emissions rates. Tree planting programs targeted to maximize energy savings will provide climate protection dividends in the Northeast.

A study of New York City's urban forest found that trees stored 1.35 million tons of atmospheric CO_2 (Nowak and Crane 2002). The 5.2 million trees sequestered approximately 42,329 tons of atmospheric CO_2 annually.

A study in Chicago focused on the carbon sequestration benefit of residential tree canopy cover. Tree canopy cover in two residential neighborhoods was estimated to sequester on average 0.112 lb/ft^2, and pruning activities released 0.016 lb/ft^2 (Jo and McPherson 1995). Net annual carbon uptake was 0.096 lb/ft^2.

A comprehensive study of CO_2 reduction by Sacramento's urban forest found the region's 6 million trees offset 1.8 percent of the total CO_2 emitted annually as a byproduct of human consumption (McPherson 1998). This savings could be substantially increased through strategic planting and long-term stewardship that maximized future energy savings from new tree plantings.

Since 1990, Trees Forever, an Iowa-based nonprofit organization, has planted trees for energy savings and atmospheric CO_2 reduction with utility sponsorships. Over 1 million trees have been planted in 400 communities with the help of 120,000 volunteers. These trees are estimated to offset CO_2 emissions by 50,000 tons annually. Based on an Iowa State University study, survival rates are an amazing 91 percent, indicating a highly trained and committed volunteer force (Ramsay 2002).

CO_2 reduction through community forestry

Improving Air Quality

Approximately 159 million people live in areas where ozone (O_3) concentrations violate federal air quality standards. About 100 million people live in areas where dust and other small particle matter (PM_{10}) exceeds levels for healthy air. Air pollution is a serious health threat to many city dwellers, causing asthma, coughing, headaches, respiratory and heart disease, and cancer (Smith 1990). Short-term increases in ozone concentrations have been statistically associated with increased mortality for 95 large U.S. cities (Bell et al. 2004). Impaired health results in increased social costs for medical care, greater absenteeism, and reduced longevity.

Nearly half of the counties with severe levels of ozone are in the Northeast region (US EPA 2005). The most severe are in the New York, New Haven, Providence, Boston, and Portland corridor along the Atlantic, the Buffalo-Rochester corridor along Lake Ontario, and western Pennsylvania (US EPA 2005). Tree planting is one practical strategy for communities in these areas to meet and sustain mandated air quality standards.

Trees improve air quality

Recently, the Environmental Protection Agency recognized tree planting as a measure for reducing O_3 in state implementation plans. Air quality management districts have funded tree planting projects to control particulate matter. These policy decisions are creating new opportunities to plant and care for trees as a method for controlling air pollution (Luley and Bond 2002, Bond 2006; for more information see www.treescleanair.org).

Urban forests provide six main air quality benefits (fig. 6):

- They absorb gaseous pollutants (e.g., O_3, nitrogen dioxide [NO_2], and sulfur dioxide [SO_2]) through leaf surfaces.

- They intercept PM_{10} (e.g., dust, ash, pollen, smoke).

- They release oxygen through photosynthesis.

- They transpire water and shade surfaces, which lowers air temperatures, thereby reducing O_3 levels.

- They reduce energy use, which reduces emissions of pollutants from power plants, including NO_2, SO_2, PM_{10}, and volatile organic compounds (**VOCs**).

- They reduce evaporative hydrocarbon emissions and O_3 formation by shading paved surfaces and parked cars.

Trees affect ozone formation

Trees can adversely affect air quality. Most trees emit **biogenic volatile organic compounds** (BVOCs) such as isoprenes and monoterpenes that can contribute to O_3 formation. The contribution of BVOC emissions from city trees to O_3 formation depends on complex geographic and atmospheric interactions that have not been studied in most cities. Some complicating factors include variations with temperature and atmospheric levels of NO_2. As well, the O_3-forming potential differs considerably for different tree species (Benjamin and Winer 1998). Genera having the greatest relative effect on increasing O_3 are sweetgum, blackgum, sycamore, poplar, and oak (Nowak 2000). A computer simulation study for Atlanta found that

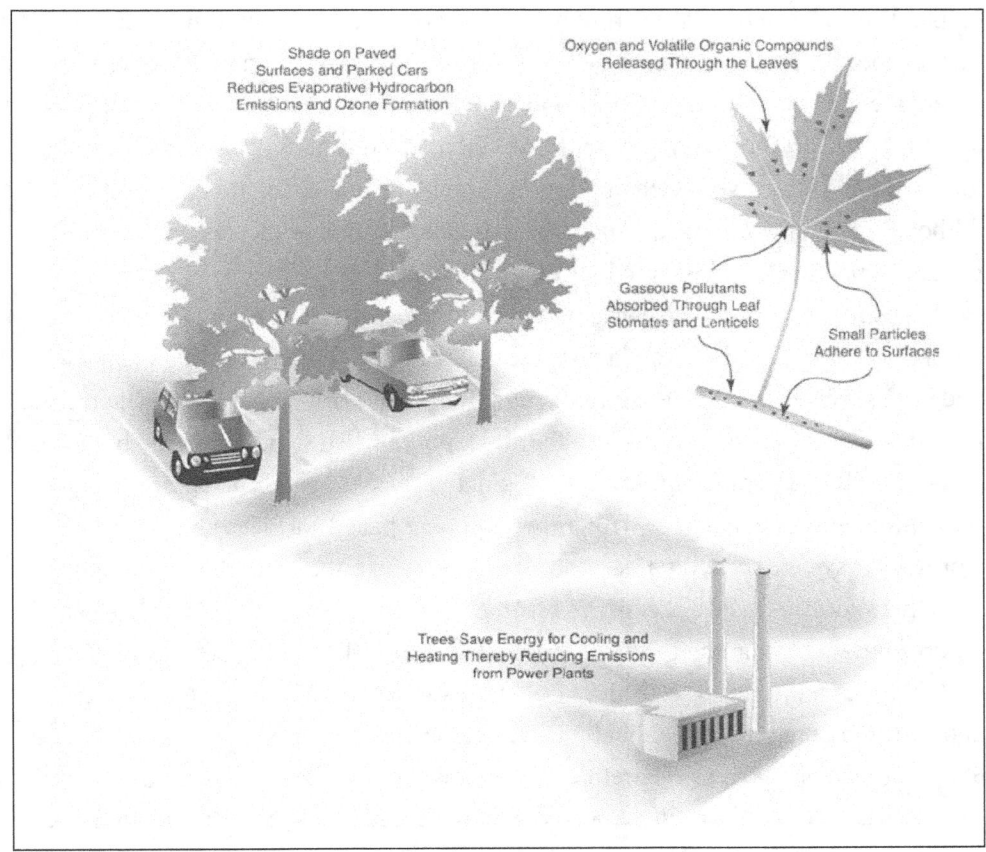

Figure 6—Trees absorb gaseous pollutants, retain particles on their surfaces, and release oxygen and volatile organic compounds. By cooling urban heat islands and shading parked cars, trees can reduce ozone formation (drawing by Mike Thomas).

it would be very difficult to meet EPA ozone standards by using trees because of the high BVOC emissions from pines and other vegetation (Chameides et al. 1988). Although removing trees reduced BVOC emissions, this effect was overwhelmed by increased hydrocarbon emissions from natural and anthropogenic sources owing to the increased air temperatures associated with tree removal (Cardelino and Chameides 1990). In the Los Angeles basin, increased planting of low BVOC-emitting tree species would reduce O_3 concentrations, whereas planting of medium- and high-emitters would increase overall O_3 concentrations (Taha 1996). A study in the Northeastern United States, however, found that species mix had no detectable effects on O_3 concentrations (Nowak et al. 2000). Although new trees increased BVOC emissions, ambient VOC emissions were so high that additional BVOCs had little effect on air quality. These potentially negative effects of trees on one kind of air pollution must be considered in light of their great benefit in other areas.

Trees absorb gaseous pollutants through leaf stomates—tiny openings in the leaves. Secondary methods of pollutant removal include adsorption of gases

Trees absorb gaseous pollutants

11

on plant surfaces and uptake through bark pores. Once gases enter the leaf, they diffuse into intercellular spaces, where some react with inner leaf surfaces and others are absorbed by water films to form acids. Pollutants can damage plants by altering their metabolism and growth. At high concentrations, pollutants cause visible damage to leaves, such as stippling and bleaching (Costello et al. 2003). Although they may pose health hazards to plants, pollutants such as nitrogenous gases can be sources of essential nutrients for trees.

Trees intercept particulate matter

Trees intercept small airborne particles. Some particles that impact a tree are absorbed, but most adhere to plant surfaces. Species with hairy or rough leaf, twig, and bark surfaces are efficient interceptors (Smith and Dochinger 1976). Intercepted particles are often resuspended into the atmosphere when wind blows the branches, and rain will wash some particulates off plant surfaces. The ultimate fate of these pollutants depends on whether they fall onto paved surfaces and enter the stormwater system, or fall on pervious surfaces, where they are filtered in the soil.

Trees release oxygen

Urban forests freshen the air we breathe by releasing oxygen as a byproduct of photosynthesis. Net annual oxygen production differs depending on tree species, size, health, and location. A healthy tree, for example, a 32-ft tall ash, produces about 260 lb of net oxygen annually (McPherson 1997). A typical person consumes 386 lb of oxygen per year. Therefore, two medium-sized, healthy trees can supply the oxygen required for a single person over the course of a year. In colder climates, oxygen release will be less than in areas with longer growing seasons.

Trees near buildings can reduce the demand for heating and air conditioning, thereby reducing emissions of PM_{10}, SO_2, NO_2, and VOCs associated with electric power production. Emissions avoided because of trees can be sizable. For example, a strategically located tree can save 100 kWh in electricity for cooling annually (McPherson and Simpson 1999, 2002, 2003). Assuming that this conserved electricity comes from a new coal-fired power plant, the tree reduces emissions of SO_2 by 0.38 lb, NO_2 by 0.27 lb, and PM_{10} by 0.84 lb (US EPA 1998). The same tree is responsible for conserving 60 gal of water in cooling towers and reducing CO_2 emissions by 200 lb.

Trees shade prevents evaporative hydrocarbon emissions

In New York City, a tree **canopy** cover of 17 percent was estimated to remove 1,973 tons of air pollution at an estimated value of $9.24 million (Nowak et al. 2006). In Charlotte, North Carolina the tree canopy (49 percent) was estimated to remove 3,591 tons of air pollutants annually with a value of $17.9 million (American Forests 2003). The urban forest of Montgomery, Alabama (33 percent tree cover), removed 1,603 tons of air pollutants valued at $7.9 million (American Forests 2004). Chicago's 50.8 million trees were estimated to remove 234 tons of PM_{10}, 210 tons of O_3, 93 tons of SO_2, and 17 tons of carbon monoxide in 1991. This environmental service was valued at $9.2 million (Nowak 1994).

Figure 7—Trees planted to shade parking areas can reduce hydrocarbon emissions and improve air quality (photo courtesy of Phillip Rodbell).

Trees in a Davis, California, parking lot were found to improve air quality by reducing air temperatures 1 to 3 °F (Scott et al. 1999). By shading asphalt surfaces and parked vehicles, trees reduce hydrocarbon emissions (VOCs) from gasoline that evaporates out of leaky fuel tanks and worn hoses (fig. 7). These evaporative emissions are a principal component of smog, and parked vehicles are a primary source. In California, parking lot tree plantings can be funded as an air quality improvement measure because of the associated reductions in evaporative emissions.

Reducing Stormwater Runoff and Improving Hydrology

Urban stormwater runoff is a major source of pollution entering wetlands, streams, lakes, and oceans. Healthy trees can reduce the amount of runoff and pollutants in receiving waters (Cappiella et al. 2005). This is important because federal law requires states and localities to control nonpoint-source pollution, such as runoff from pavements, buildings, and landscapes. Also, many older cities have combined sewer outflow systems, and during large rain events excess runoff can mix with raw sewage. Rainfall interception by trees can reduce the magnitude of this problem during large storms. Trees are mini-reservoirs, controlling runoff at the source, thereby reducing runoff volumes and erosion of watercourses, as well as delaying the onset of peak flows. Trees can reduce runoff in several ways (fig. 8):

- Leaves and branch surfaces intercept and store rainfall, thereby reducing runoff volumes and delaying the onset of peak flows.

- Roots increase the rate at which rainfall infiltrates soil and the capacity of soil to store water, reducing overland flow.

- Tree canopies reduce soil erosion by diminishing the impact of raindrops on barren surfaces.

- Transpiration through tree leaves reduces soil moisture, increasing the soil's capacity to store rainfall.

Rainfall that is stored temporarily on canopy leaf and bark surfaces is called intercepted rainfall. Intercepted water evaporates, drips from leaf surfaces, and flows down stem surfaces to the ground. Tree-surface saturation generally occurs

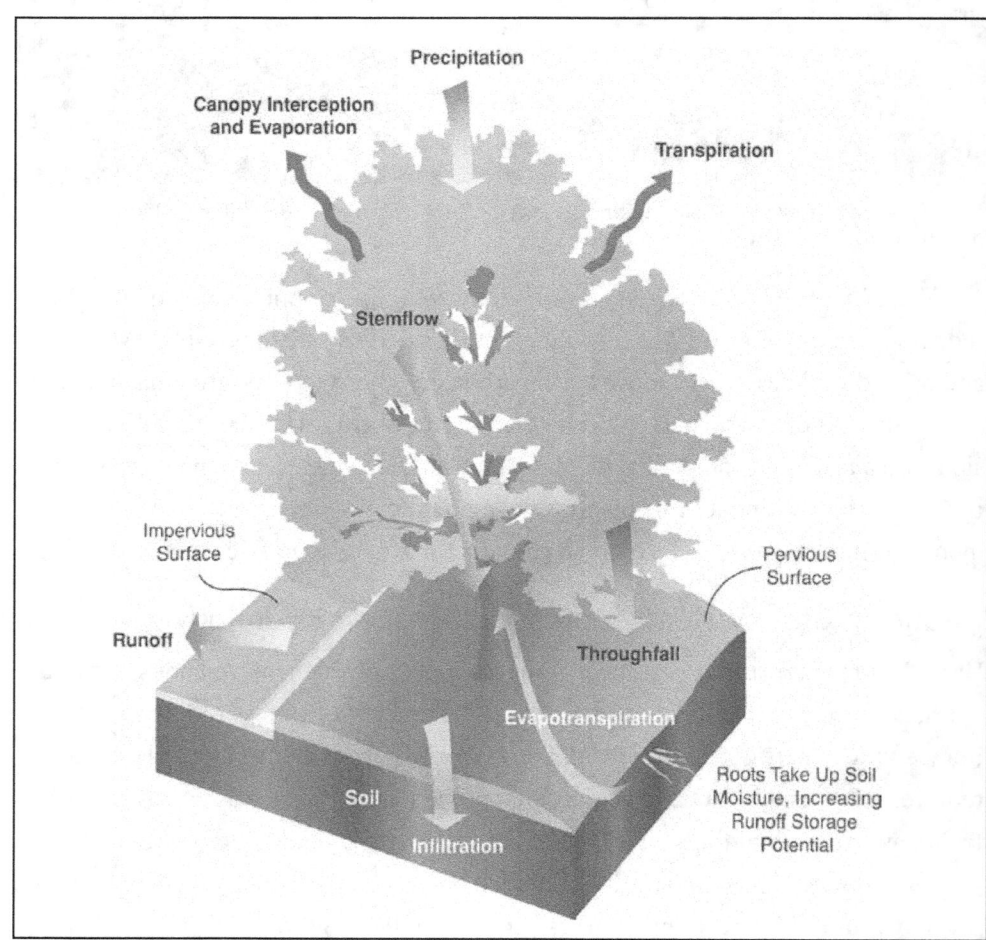

Figure 8—Trees intercept a portion of rainfall that then evaporates and never reaches the ground. Some rainfall runs to the ground along branches and stems (stemflow), and some falls through gaps or drips off leaves and branches (throughfall). Transpiration increases soil moisture storage potential (drawing by Mike Thomas).

after 1 to 2 in of rainfall has fallen (Xiao et al. 2000). During large storm events, rainfall exceeds the amount that the tree crown can store, about 50 to 100 gal per tree. The interception benefit is the amount of rainfall that does not reach the ground because it evaporates from the crown. As a result, the volume of runoff is reduced and the time of peak flow is delayed. Trees protect water quality by substantially reducing runoff during small rainfall events that are responsible for most pollutant washoff. Therefore, urban forests generally produce more benefits through water quality protection than through flood control (Xiao et al. 1998, 2000).

The amount of rainfall trees intercept depends on their architecture, rainfall patterns, and climate. Tree-crown characteristics that influence interception are the trunk, stem, and surface areas, textures, area of gaps, period when leaves are present, and dimensions (e.g., tree height and diameter). Trees with coarse surfaces retain more rainfall than those with smooth surfaces. Large trees generally intercept more rainfall than small trees do because greater surface areas allow for greater evaporation rates. Tree crowns with few gaps reduce throughfall to the ground. Species that are in leaf when rainfall is plentiful are more effective than deciduous species that have dropped their leaves during the rainy season.

Studies that have simulated urban forest effects on stormwater runoff have reported reductions of 2 to 7 percent. Annual interception of rainfall by Sacramento's urban forest for the total urbanized area was only about 2 percent because of the winter rainfall pattern and lack of **evergreen** species (Xiao et al. 1998). However, average interception under the tree canopy ranged from 6 to 13 percent (150 gal per tree), close to values reported for rural forests. Broadleaf evergreens and **conifers** intercept more rainfall than deciduous species in areas where rainfall is highest in fall, winter, or spring (Xiao and McPherson 2002).

In Montgomery, Alabama, tree canopy (33 percent) reduced runoff by 227 million ft^3, valued at \$454 million per 20-year construction cycle (American Forests 2004). In Charlotte, North Carolina, the existing canopy (49 percent) reduced runoff by 398 million ft^3, with an estimated value of \$797 million (American Forests 2003).

Urban forests can provide other hydrologic benefits, too. For example, tree plantations or nurseries can be irrigated with partially treated wastewater. Infiltration of water through the soil can be a safe and productive means of water treatment. Reused wastewater applied to urban forest lands can recharge aquifers, reduce stormwater-treatment loads, and create income through sales of nursery or wood products. Recycling urban wastewater into greenspace areas can be an economical means of treatment and disposal while at the same time providing other environmental benefits (USDA NRCS 2005).

Trees reduce runoff

Urban forests can treat wastewater

Aesthetics and Other Benefits

Beautification

Trees provide a host of aesthetic, social, economic, and health benefits that should be included in any benefit-cost analysis. One of the most frequently cited reasons that people plant trees is for beautification. Trees add color, texture, line, and form to the landscape. In this way, trees soften the hard geometry that dominates built environments. Research on the aesthetic quality of residential streets has shown that street trees are the single strongest positive influence on scenic quality (Schroeder and Cannon 1983).

Attractiveness of retail settings

Consumer surveys have found that preference ratings increase with the presence of trees in the commercial streetscape. In contrast to areas without trees, shoppers shop more often and longer in well-landscaped business districts. They were willing to pay more for parking and up to 11 percent more for goods and services (Wolf 2005).

Public safety benefits

Research in public housing complexes found that outdoor spaces with trees were used significantly more often than spaces without trees. By facilitating interactions among residents, trees can contribute to reduced levels of domestic violence, as well as foster safer and more sociable neighborhood environments (Sullivan and Kuo 1996).

Property value benefits

Well-maintained trees increase the "curb appeal" of properties (fig. 9). Research comparing sales prices of residential properties with different numbers of trees suggests that people are willing to pay 3 to 7 percent more for properties with ample trees versus few or no trees. One of the most comprehensive studies of the influence of trees on residential property values was based on actual sales prices and found that each large front-yard tree was associated with about a 1-percent increase in sales price (Anderson and Cordell 1988). A much greater value of 9 percent ($15,000) was determined in a U.S. Tax Court case for the loss of a large black oak on a property valued at $164,500 (Neely 1988). Depending on average home sales prices, the value of this benefit can contribute significantly to cities' property tax revenues.

Social and psychological benefits

Scientific studies confirm our intuition that trees in cities provide social and psychological benefits. Humans derive substantial pleasure from trees, whether it is inspiration from their beauty, a spiritual connection, or a sense of meaning (Dwyer et al. 1992, Lewis 1996). Following natural disasters, people often report a sense of loss if their community forest has been damaged (Hull 1992). Views of trees and nature from homes and offices provide restorative experiences that ease mental fatigue and help people to concentrate (Kaplan and Kaplan 1989). Desk workers with a view of nature report lower rates of sickness and greater satisfaction with their jobs compared to those having no visual connection to nature (Kaplan 1992).

Figure 9—Trees beautify a neighborhood, increasing property values and creating a more sociable environment (photo courtesy of Phillip Rodbell).

Trees provide important settings for recreation and relaxation in and near cities. The act of planting trees can have social value, as bonds between people and local groups often result.

Human health benefits

The presence of trees in cities provides public health benefits and improves the well-being of those who live, work, and play in cities. Physical and emotional stress has both short-term and long-term effects. Prolonged stress can compromise the human immune system. A series of studies on human stress caused by general urban conditions and city driving show that views of nature reduce the stress response of both body and mind (Parsons et al. 1998). Urban green also appears to have an "immunization effect," in that people show less stress response if they have had a recent view of trees and vegetation. Hospitalized patients with views of nature and time spent outdoors need less medication, sleep better, have a better outlook, and recover more quickly than patients without connections to nature (Ulrich 1985). Skin cancer is a particular concern in the sunny Northeast region. Trees reduce exposure to ultraviolet light, thereby lowering the risk of harmful effects from skin cancer and cataracts (Tretheway and Manthe 1999).

Noise reduction

Certain environmental benefits from trees are more difficult to quantify than those previously described, but can be just as important. Noise can reach unhealthy levels in cities. Trucks, trains, and planes can produce noise that exceeds 100 decibels, twice the level at which noise becomes a health risk. Thick strips of vegetation

17

in conjunction with landforms or solid barriers can reduce highway noise by 6 to 15 decibels. Plants absorb more high-frequency noise than low frequency, which is advantageous to humans, as higher frequencies are most distressing to people (Cook 1978).

Wildlife habitat

Numerous types of wildlife inhabit cities and are generally highly valued by residents. For example, older parks, cemeteries, and botanical gardens often contain a rich assemblage of wildlife. Remnant woodlands and **riparian habitats** within cities can connect a city to its surrounding bioregion (fig. 10). Wetlands, greenways (linear parks), and other greenspace can provide habitats that conserve **biodiversity** (Platt et al. 1994). Native plants are particularly valuable because they support wildlife. Also, regionally appropriate and native plant selections reduce potential resource inputs.

Jobs and environmental education

Urban forestry can provide jobs for both skilled and unskilled labor. Public service programs and grassroots-led urban and community forestry programs provide horticultural training to volunteers across the United States. Also, urban and community forestry provides educational opportunities for residents who want to learn about nature through first-hand experience (McPherson and Mathis 1999).

Figure 10—Natural areas within cities are refuges for wildlife and help connect city dwellers with their ecosystems.

Figure 11—Although shade trees can be expensive to maintain, their shade can reduce the costs of resurfacing streets (McPherson and Muchnick 2005), promote pedestrian travel, and improve air quality directly through pollutant uptake and indirectly through reduced emissions of volatile organic compounds from cars.

Local nonprofit tree groups and municipal volunteer programs often provide educational material and hands-on training in the care of trees and work with area schools.

Tree shade on streets can help offset pavement management costs by protecting paving from weathering. The asphalt paving on streets contains stone aggregate in an oil binder. Tree shade lowers the street surface temperature and reduces heating and volatilization of the binder (McPherson and Muchnick 2005). As a result, the aggregate remains protected for a longer period by the oil binder. When unprotected, vehicles loosen the aggregate, and much like sandpaper, the loose aggregate grinds down the pavement. Because most weathering of asphalt-concrete pavement occurs during the first 5 to 10 years, when new street tree plantings provide little shade, this benefit mainly applies when older streets are resurfaced (fig. 11).

Shade can reduce street maintenance

Costs

Planting and Maintaining Trees

The environmental, social, and economic benefits of urban and community forests come at a price. A national survey reported that communities in the Northeast region spent an average of about $1.94 per tree, in 1994, for street- and park-tree management (Tschantz and Sacamano 1994). This amount is relatively low, with eight national regions spending more than this and two regions spending less. Nationwide, the single largest expenditure was for tree pruning, followed by tree removal/disposal, and tree planting.

Municipal costs of tree care

Our survey of **municipal foresters** in Fairfield and Mansfield, Connecticut, and New York City, indicates that they are spending about $20 to $30 per tree annually. Most of this amount is for pruning ($6 to $12 per tree), planting ($10 per tree), removal and disposal ($2 per tree), and administration ($4 to $7 per tree). Other municipal departments incur costs for infrastructure repair and trip-and-fall claims that average about $2 per tree annually.

Frequently, trees in new residential subdivisions are planted by developers, whereas cities and counties and volunteer groups plant trees on existing streets and parklands. In some cities, tree planting has not kept pace with removals. Moreover, limited growing space in cities or preferences for flowering trees results in increased planting of smaller, shorter lived species that provide fewer benefits than larger trees do.

Residential costs differ

Annual expenditures for tree management on private property have not been well documented. Costs differ considerably, ranging from some commercial or residential properties that receive regular professional landscape service to others that are virtually "wild" and without maintenance. An analysis of data for Sacramento suggested that households typically spent about $5 to $10 annually per tree for pruning and pest and disease control (Summit and McPherson 1998). Our survey of commercial arborists in the Northeast indicated that expenditures typically range from $20 to $40 per tree. Expenditures are usually greatest for planting, pruning, and removal.

Conflicts With Urban Infrastructure

Tree roots can damage sidewalks

Like other cities across the United States, communities in the Northeast region are spending millions of dollars each year to manage conflicts between trees and power lines, sidewalks, sewers, and other elements of the urban infrastructure (Randrup et al. 2001a). In 2004, New York City began to address conflicts between trees and sidewalks and currently spends $3 million a year (about $6 per tree) on the repair of sidewalks damaged by tree roots. This amount is less than the $11.22 per tree reported for 18 California cities (McPherson 2000). As well, the figures for California apply only to street trees and do not include repair costs for damaged sewer lines, building foundations, parking lots, and various other **hardscape** elements.

In some Northeast cities, tree growth and deteriorating infrastructure in tight municipal budget times are causing some cities to shift repair costs to homeowners. This shift has significant impacts on residents in older areas, where large trees have outgrown small sites and infrastructure has deteriorated. It should be noted that trees should not always bear full responsibility. In older areas, in particular, sidewalks and curbs may have reached the end of their 20- to 25-year service life or may have been poorly constructed in the first place (Sydnor et al. 2000).

Efforts to control the costs of these conflicts are having alarming effects on urban forests (Bernhardt and Swiecki 1993, Thompson and Ahern 2000):

Costs of conflicts

- Cities are downsizing their municipal forests by planting smaller trees. Although small trees are appropriate under power lines and in small planting sites, they are less effective than large trees at providing shade, absorbing air pollutants, and intercepting rainfall.

- Sidewalk damage was the second most common reason that street and park trees were removed. Thousands of healthy urban trees are lost each year and their benefits forgone because of this problem.

- Most cities surveyed were removing more trees than they were planting. Residents forced to pay for sidewalk repairs may not want replacement trees.

Cost-effective strategies to retain benefits from large street trees while reducing costs associated with infrastructure conflicts are described in *Reducing Infrastructure Damage by Tree Roots* (Costello and Jones 2003). Matching the growth characteristics of trees to the conditions at the planting site is one important strategy. Other strategies include meandering sidewalks around trees, suspending sidewalks above tree roots, and replacing concrete sidewalks with recycled rubber sidewalks.

Tree roots can also damage old sewer lines that are cracked or otherwise susceptible to invasion (Randrup et al. 2001b). Sewer repair companies estimate that sewer damage is minor until trees and sewers are over 30 years old, and roots from trees in yards are usually more of a problem than roots from trees in planter strips along streets. The latter assertion may be due to the fact that sewers are closer to the root zone as they enter houses than at the street. Repair costs typically range from $100 for sewer rodding (inserting a cleaning implement to temporarily remove roots) to $1,000 or more for sewer excavation and replacement.

Cleaning up after trees

Most communities sweep their streets regularly to reduce surface-runoff pollution entering local waterways. Street trees drop leaves, flowers, fruit, and branches year round that constitute a significant portion of debris collected from city streets. When leaves fall and winter rains begin, **tree litter** can clog sewers, dry wells, and other elements of flood-control systems. Costs include additional labor needed to remove leaves, and property damage caused by localized flooding. Windstorms also incur cleanup costs. Although serious natural catastrophes are infrequent, they can result in large expenditures.

Large trees under power lines can be costly

The cost of addressing conflicts between trees and power lines is reflected in electric rates. Large trees under power lines require frequent pruning, which can make them unattractive (fig. 12). Frequent crown reduction reduces the benefits these trees could otherwise provide. Moreover, increased costs for pruning are passed on to customers.

Wood Salvage, Recycling, and Disposal

Recycling green waste may pay for itself

According to our survey, most Northeast cities are recycling green waste from urban trees as mulch, compost, and firewood. Some power plants will use this wood to generate electricity, thereby helping defray costs for hauling and grinding. Generally, the net costs of waste-wood disposal are less than 1 percent of total tree-care costs, and cities and contractors may break even. Hauling and recycling costs are nearly offset by revenues from sales of mulch, milled lumber, and firewood. The cost of wood disposal may be higher depending on geographic location and the presence of exotic pests that require elaborate waste-wood disposal.

Figure 12—Large trees planted under power lines can require extensive pruning, which increases tree care costs and reduces the benefits of those trees, including their appearance.

Chapter 3. Determining Benefits and Costs of Community Forests in Northeast Communities

This chapter presents estimated benefits and costs for trees planted in typical residential yards and public sites. Because benefits and costs vary with tree size, we report results for representative small, medium, and large deciduous trees and for a representative conifer.

Estimates of benefits and costs are initial approximations, as some benefits and costs are intangible or difficult to quantify (e.g., impacts on psychological health, crime, and violence). Limited knowledge about the physical processes at work and their interactions makes estimates imprecise (e.g., fate of air pollutants trapped by trees and then washed to the ground by rainfall). Tree growth and mortality rates are highly variable throughout the region. Benefits and costs also vary, depending on differences in climate, air pollutant concentrations, tree-maintenance practices, and other factors. Given the Northeast region's large geographical area, with many different climates, soils, and types of community forestry programs, the approach used here provides first-order approximations. It is a general accounting that can be easily adapted and adjusted for local planting projects. It provides a basis for decisions that set priorities and influence management direction (Maco and McPherson 2003).

Overview of Procedures

Approach

In this study, annual benefits and costs are estimated over a 40-year planning horizon for newly planted trees in three residential yard locations (about 27 ft from the east, south, and west walls of the residence) and a public streetside or park location. Henceforth, we refer to trees in these hypothetical locations as "yard" trees and "public" trees, respectively. Prices are assigned to each cost (e.g., planting, pruning, removal, irrigation, infrastructure repair, liability) and benefit (e.g., heating/cooling energy savings, air pollutant mitigation, stormwater runoff reduction, property value increase) through direct estimation and implied valuation of benefits as environmental externalities. This approach makes it possible to estimate the net benefits of plantings in "typical" locations using "typical" tree species. More information on data collection, modeling procedures, and assumptions can be found in appendix C.

To account for differences in the mature size and growth of different tree species, we report results for a small deciduous tree, the Kwanzan cherry (see "Common and Scientific Names" section), a medium deciduous tree, the red maple, a large deciduous tree, the Japanese zelkova, and a conifer, the eastern white pine (figs. 13 through 16). The conifer is included as a windbreak tree located more than 50 ft from the residence so it does not shade the building. Tree dimensions are

Figure 13—The Kwanzan cherry represents small deciduous trees in this guide.

Figure 14—The red maple represents medium deciduous trees in this guide.

Figure 15—The Japanese zelkova represents large deciduous trees in this guide.

Figure 16—The eastern white pine represents coniferous trees in this guide.

derived from growth curves developed from street trees in the Borough of Queens, New York City (Peper et al., in press.) (fig. 17). The selection of these species was based on data availability and not intended to endorse their use in large numbers. In fact, the Kwanzan cherry has a poor form for a street tree, and in certain areas zelkova is overused. Relying on too few species can increase the likelihood of catastrophic loss owing to pests, disease, or other threat.

Tree care costs based on survey findings

Frequency and costs of tree management are estimated based on surveys with municipal foresters from Fairfield and Mansfield, Connecticut, and New York City. In addition, commercial arborists from the metropolitan New York region provided information on tree-management costs on residential properties.

Tree benefits based on numerical models

Benefits are calculated with numerical models and data from the region (e.g., pollutant emission factors for avoided emissions owing to energy savings) and from local sources (e.g., New York City climate data for energy effects). Regional electricity and natural gas prices are used in this study to quantify energy savings. Costs of preventing or repairing damage from pollution, flooding, or other environmental risks were used to estimate society's **willingness to pay** for clean air and water (Wang and Santini 1995). For example, the value of stormwater runoff reduction owing to rainfall interception by trees is estimated by using marginal control costs. If a community or developer is willing to pay an average of $0.01 per gal of treated and controlled runoff to meet minimum standards, then the stormwater runoff mitigation value of a tree that intercepts 1,000 gal of rainfall, eliminating the need for control, should be $10.

Reporting Results

Tree mortality included

Results are reported in terms of annual value per tree planted. To make these calculations realistic, however, mortality rates are included. Based on our survey of regional municipal foresters and commercial arborists, this analysis assumes that 34 percent of the planted trees will die over the 40-year period. Annual mortality rates are 2.8 percent per year for the first 5 years and 0.57 percent per year for the remainder of the 40-year period. This accounting approach "grows" trees in different locations and uses computer simulation to directly calculate the annual flow of benefits and costs as trees mature and die (McPherson 1992). In appendix 2, results are reported at 5-year intervals for 40 years.

Findings of This Study

Average annual net benefits increase with tree size

Average Annual Net Benefits

Average annual net benefits (benefits minus costs) per tree increase with mature tree size (for detailed results see app. 2):

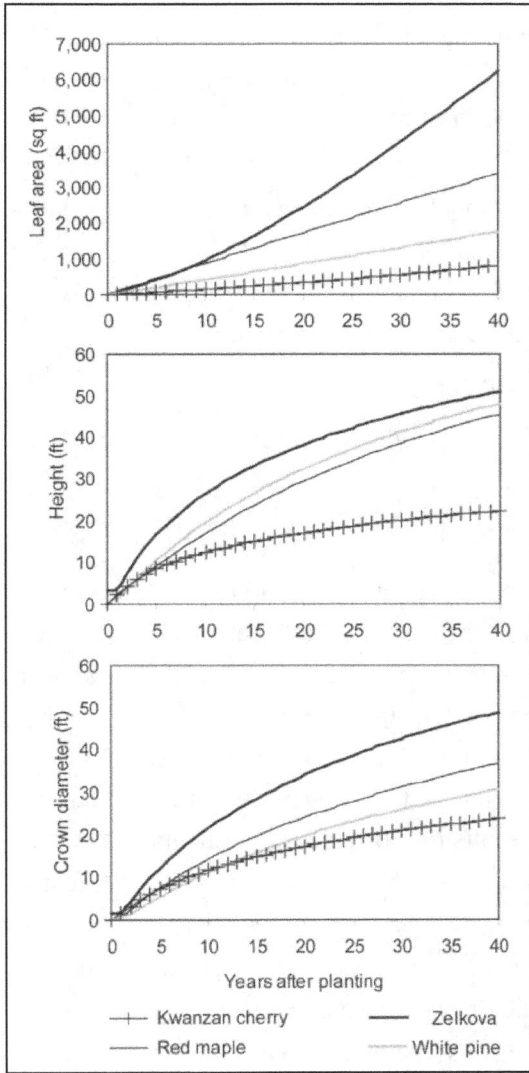

Figure 17—Tree growth curves are based on data collected from street trees in New York City, New York. Data for representative small, medium, and large deciduous trees and conifer trees are for the Kwanzan cherry, red maple, Japanese zelkova, and eastern white pine, respectively. Differences in leaf surface area among species are most important for this analysis because functional benefits such as summer shade, rainfall interception, and pollutant uptake are related to leaf area.

- $5 to $9 for a small tree
- $36 to $52 for a medium tree
- $85 to $113 for a large tree
- $21 to $33 for a conifer

Our findings demonstrate that average annual net benefits from large trees, like the Japanese zelkova, can be substantially greater than those from small trees like Kwanzan cherry. Average annual net benefits for the small, medium, and large deciduous public trees are $9, $52, and $113, respectively. Conifers provide an intermediate level of benefits, on average $33 for a public tree. The largest average annual net benefits from yard trees stemmed from a tree opposite the west-facing wall of a house: $8, $46, and $107 for small, medium, and large deciduous trees, respectively. The pine tree windbreak provides an average annual net benefit of $21 per tree regardless of location because it is too far away to shade the residence.

Large trees provide the most benefits

27

Net annual benefits at year 40

The large yard tree opposite a west wall produces a net annual benefit of $155 at year 40. In the same location, 40 years after planting, the cherry, red maple, and white pine produce annual net benefits of $26, $77, and $46, respectively.

Forty years after planting at a typical public site, the small, medium, and large deciduous trees and the conifer provide annual net benefits of $27, $73, $154, and $53, respectively.

Net benefits summed over 40 years

Net benefits for a yard tree opposite a west house wall and a public tree also increase with size when summed over the entire 40-year period:

- $320 (yard) and $364 (public) for a small tree
- $1,849 (yard) and $2,066 (public) for a medium tree
- $4,261 (yard) and $4,531 (public) for a large tree
- $855 (yard) and $1,322 (public) for a conifer

Year 20: environmental benefits exceed tree care costs

Twenty years after planting, average annual benefits for all trees exceed costs of tree planting and management (tables 1 and 2). For a large zelkova in a yard 20 years after planting, the total value of environmental benefits alone ($92) is almost five times the total annual cost ($21). Environmental benefits total $22, $46, and $36 for the flowering cherry, red maple, and white pine, whereas tree care costs are lower, $5, $19, and $17, respectively. Adding the value of aesthetics and other benefits to the environmental benefits results in substantial net benefits.

Net benefits are slightly less for yard trees (table 2) than public trees because tree care costs are greater. Based on our survey findings, private yard trees are more expensive to plant than public trees and are pruned more frequently. The standard of care is often lower for public trees because municipal budgets tend to reflect what is allocated, not what is needed to maintain a healthy urban forest.

Average Annual Costs

Costs of tree care

Averaged over 40 years, the costs for yard and public trees, are as follows:

- $22 (yard) and $20 (public) for a small tree
- $33 (yard) and $27 (public) for a medium tree
- $40 (yard) and $34 (public) for a large tree
- $33 (yard) and $23 (public) for a conifer

Costs increase with mature tree size because of added expenses for pruning and removing larger trees.

Over the 40-year period, tree planting is the single greatest cost for public trees, averaging approximately $10 to $15 per tree per year (see app. 2). Based on our survey, we assume in this study that a yard tree with a 2-in **diameter at breast**

Table 1—Estimated annual benefits and costs for a private tree (residential yard) opposite the west-facing wall 20 years after planting

Benefit category	Kwanzan cherry small tree 17 ft tall 17-ft spread LSA = 338 ft²		Red maple medium tree 29 ft tall 24-ft spread LSA = 1,725 ft²		Japanese zelkova large tree 38 ft tall 34-ft spread LSA = 2,510 ft²		Eastern white pine conifer 32 ft tall 20-ft spread LSA = 861 ft²	
	Resource units	Total value	Resource units	Total value	Resource units	Total value	Resource units	Total value
		Dollars		*Dollars*		*Dollars*		*Dollars*
Electricity savings ($0.1401/kWh)	27 kWh	3.72	71 kWh	9.95	176 kWh	24.73	22 kWh	3.05
Natural gas savings ($0.0148/kBtu)	797 kBtu	11.79	1,450 kBtu	21.47	2,768 kBtu	40.97	1,507 kBtu	22.30
Carbon dioxide ($0.00334/lb)	145 lb	0.48	271 lb	0.91	563 lb	1.88	211 lb	0.70
Ozone ($4.59/lb)	0.13 lb	0.58	0.24 lb	1.12	0.49 lb	2.24	0.23 lb	1.07
Nitrogen dioxide ($4.59/lb)	0.17 lb	0.78	0.33 lb	1.54	0.70 lb	3.21	0.30 lb	1.39
Sulfur dioxide ($3.48/lb)	0.14 lb	0.50	0.35 lb	1.22	0.87 lb	3.04	0.19 lb	0.67
Small particulate matter ($8.31/lb)	0.14 lb	1.20	0.26 lb	2.17	0.37 lb	3.06	0.37 lb	3.04
Volatile organic compounds ($2.31/lb)	0.01 lb	0.03	0.03 lb	0.07	0.07 lb	0.16	0.02 lb	0.04
Biogenic volatile organic compounds ($2.31/lb)	0.00 lb	0.00	-0.12 lb	-0.27	0.00 lb	0.00	-1.08 lb	-2.49
Rainfall interception ($0.008/gal)	312 gal	2.49	1,014 gal	8.11	1,624 gal	12.99	786 gal	6.29
Environmental subtotal		21.57		46.26		92.29		36.05
Other benefits		7.05		29.84		58.46		15.82
Total benefits		28.62		76.10		150.75		51.87
Total costs		4.93		18.88		20.81		16.51
Net benefit		23.69		57.23		129.94		35.36

LSA = leaf surface area.

Table 2—Estimated annual benefits and costs for a public tree (street/park) 20 years after planting

Benefit category	Kwanzan cherry small tree 17 ft tall 17-ft spread LSA = 338 ft²		Red maple medium tree 29 ft tall 24-ft spread LSA = 1,725 ft²		Japanese zelkova large tree 38 ft tall 34-ft spread LSA = 2,510 ft²		Eastern white pine conifer 32 ft tall 20-ft spread LSA = 861 ft²	
	Resource units	Total value	Resource units	Total value	Resource units	Total value	Resource units	Total value
		Dollars		*Dollars*		*Dollars*		*Dollars*
Electricity savings ($0.1401/kWh)	16 kWh	2.18	33 kWh	4.62	89 kWh	12.47	21.8 kWh	3.05
Natural gas savings ($0.0148/kBtu)	823 kBtu	12.18	1,534 kBtu	22.71	3,076 kBtu	45.53	1,506.8 kBtu	22.30
Carbon dioxide ($0.00334/lb)	136.76 lb	0.46	241.93 lb	0.81	508.70 lb	1.70	210.75 lb	0.70
Ozone ($4.59/lb)	0.13 lb	0.58	0.24 lb	1.12	0.49 lb	2.24	0.23 lb	1.07
Nitrogen dioxide ($4.59/lb)	0.17 lb	0.78	0.33 lb	1.54	0.70 lb	3.21	0.30 lb	1.39
Sulfur dioxide ($3.48/lb)	0.14 lb	0.50	0.35 lb	1.22	0.87 lb	3.04	0.19 lb	0.67
Small particulate matter ($8.31/lb)	0.14 lb	1.20	0.26 lb	2.17	0.37 lb	3.06	0.37 lb	3.04
Volatile organic compounds ($2.31/lb)	0.01 lb	0.03	0.03 lb	0.07	0.07 lb	0.16	0.02 lb	0.04
Biogenic volatile organic compounds ($2.31/lb)	0.00 lb	0.00	0.00 lb	-0.27	0.00 lb	0.00	-1.08 lb	-2.49
Rainfall interception ($0.008/gal)	312 gal	2.49	1,014 gal	8.11	1,624 gal	12.99		6.29
Environmental subtotal		20.38		42.08		84.42		36.06
Other benefits		7.90		33.41		65.47		17.71
Total benefits		28.28		75.49		149.89		53.77
Total costs		9.27		14.56		17.78		11.81
Net benefit		19.01		60.93		132.11		41.96

LSA = leaf surface area.

height (d.b.h.) is planted at a cost of $600, or $15 per year. The cost for planting a 2-in public tree is $400 or $10 per tree per year. Annualized expenditures for tree pruning are the second most important cost, especially for trees planted in private yards ($4 to $18 per tree per year).

Table 3 shows annual management costs 20 years after planting for yard trees to the west of a house and for public trees. Annual costs for yard trees range from $5 to $21, whereas public tree care costs are $9 to $18.

Average Annual Benefits

Average annual benefits, including energy savings, stormwater runoff reduction, aesthetic value, air quality improvement and carbon dioxide (CO_2) sequestration increase with mature tree size (figs. 18 and 19, for detailed results see app. 2):

- $26 to $30 for a small tree
- $69 to $79 for a medium tree
- $125 to $147 for a large tree
- $54 to $56 for a conifer

Energy savings—

In the Northeast region, trees provide significant energy benefits that tend to increase with tree size. For example, average annual net energy benefits are $16 for the small Kwanzan cherry opposite a west-facing wall, and $62 for the larger zelkova. Average annual net energy benefits for public trees are slightly less than for yard trees because public trees are assumed to provide general climate effects but do not shade buildings as effectively. Benefits range from $15 for the cherry to $55 for the zelkova. For species of all sizes, energy savings increase as trees mature and their leaf surface areas increase (figs. 18 and 19).

As expected in a region with temperate summers and cold winters, heating savings account for most of the total energy benefit. Although deciduous trees are leafless during the heating season, they still reduce windspeed and infiltration of cold air. Average annual heating savings for the Kwanzan cherry and zelkova range from $10 to $12 and $25 to $43, respectively. The eastern white pine in a windbreak reduces heating costs by $23 on average. Average annual cooling savings for the cherry and zelkova range from $2 to $4 and $12 to $23, respectively.

Average annual net energy benefits for residential trees are greatest for a tree located west of a building because the effect of shade on cooling costs is maximized. A yard tree located south of a building produces the least net energy benefit because it has the least benefit during summer and the greatest adverse effect on heating costs from shade in winter (see also fig. 4). Trees located east of a building

Energy benefits are crucial

Table 3—Estimated annual costs 20 years after planting for a private tree opposite the west-facing wall and a public tree

Costs	Kwanzan cherry small tree 17 ft tall 17-ft spread LSA = 338 ft²		Red maple medium tree 29 ft tall 24-ft spread LSA = 1,725 ft²		Japanese zelkova large tree 38 ft tall 34-ft spread LSA = 2,510 ft²		Eastern white pine conifer 32 ft tall 20-ft spread LSA = 861 ft²	
	Private: west	Public tree	Private: west	Public tree	Private: west	Public tree	Private: west	Public tree
	Dollars per year per tree							
Tree and planting	0.00	0.00	0.00	0.00	0.00	0.00	0.00	0.00
Pruning	0.98	2.71	13.38	5.42	13.38	5.42	13.38	5.42
Remove and dispose	2.34	0.97	3.25	1.35	4.40	1.82	2.91	1.20
Pest and disease	0.00	0.10	0.00	0.14	0.00	0.18	0.00	0.12
Infrastructure	0.15	1.16	0.20	1.62	0.27	2.19	0.18	1.45
Irrigation	0.00	0.00	0.00	0.00	0.00	0.00	0.00	0.00
Cleanup	0.03	0.26	0.05	0.37	0.06	0.49	0.04	0.33
Liability and legal	0.00	0.00	0.00	0.00	0.00	0.00	0.00	0.00
Admin. and other	1.43	4.07	1.99	5.67	2.70	7.67	0.00	3.29
Total costs	4.93	9.27	18.88	14.56	20.81	17.78	16.51	11.81
Total benefits	29.22	28.85	77.23	76.50	153.09	152.01	52.75	54.65
Net benefit	24.29	19.58	58.35	61.94	132.28	134.23	36.24	42.84

Note: Prices for removal and disposal are included to account for expected mortality of citywide planting.
LSA = leaf surface area.

provide intermediate net benefits. Net energy benefits also reflect species-related traits such as size, form, branch pattern and density, and time in leaf.

Stormwater runoff reduction—

Benefits associated with rainfall interception, reducing stormwater runoff, are substantial for all tree types. The Kwanzan cherry intercepts 358 gal/year on average over a 40-year period with an estimated annual value of $3. The red maple, zelkova, and white pine intercept 1,156 gal/year, 1,909 gal/year, and 909 gal/year on average, with annual values of $9, $15, and $7, respectively.

As metropolitan areas in the Northeast grow, the amount of impervious surface increases. The role that trees can play in protecting water quality by reducing stormwater runoff is substantial.

Aesthetic and other benefits—

Benefits associated with property value account for the second largest portion of total benefits. As trees grow and become more visible, they can increase a property's sales price. Average annual values associated with these aesthetic and other benefits for yard trees are $7, $29, $55, and $15 for the small, medium, and large deciduous trees and for the conifer, respectively. The values for public trees are $8, $33, $62, and $17, respectively. The values for yard trees are slightly less than for public trees because off-street trees contribute less to a property's curb appeal than more prominent street trees. Because our estimates are based on

Aesthetic benefits are substantial

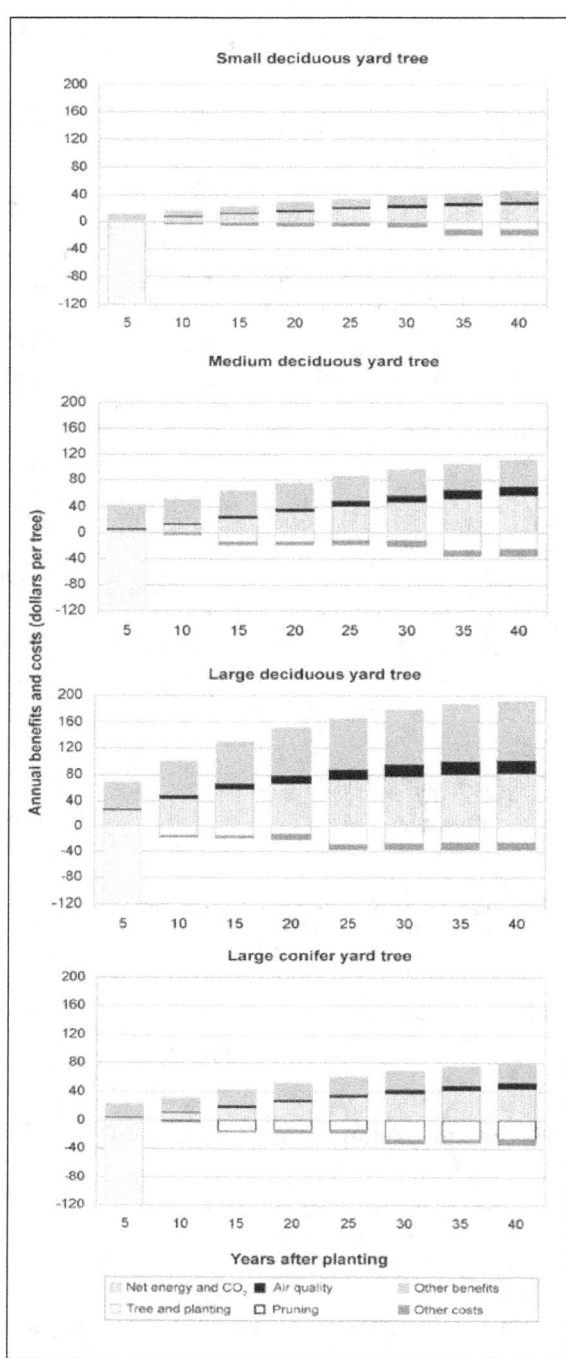

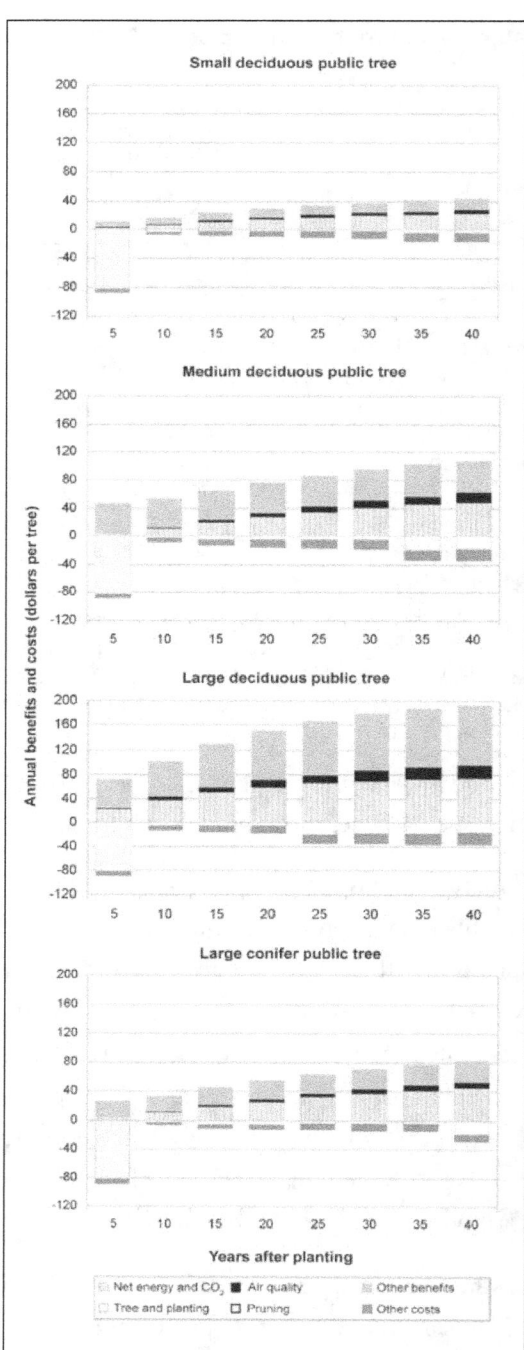

Figure 18— Estimated annual benefits and costs for a small (Kwanzan cherry), medium (red maple), and large (zelkova) deciduous tree, and a conifer (eastern white pine) located west of a residence. Costs are greatest during the initial establishment period, and benefits increase with tree size.

Figure 19— Estimated annual benefits and costs for public small (Kwanzan cherry), medium (red maple), and large (zelkova) deciduous trees, and a public conifer (eastern white pine).

median home sale prices, the effects of trees on property values and aesthetics will vary depending on local economies.

Carbon dioxide reduction—

Net atmospheric CO_2 reductions accrue for all tree types. Average annual net reductions range from a high of 532 lbs ($1.78) for a large tree on the west side of a house to a low of 129 lbs ($0.43) for the small tree on the southern side of the house. Deciduous trees opposite west-facing house walls produced the greatest CO_2 reduction owing to avoided power plant emissions associated with energy savings. The values for the Kwanzan cherry are lowest for CO_2 reduction because of the relatively small impacts of shade and windspeed reduction from the small-growing tree on energy consumption.

Forty years after planting, average annual avoided emissions and sequestered and released CO_2 for a yard tree opposite a west wall are 252, 462, 686, and 364 lbs, respectively, for the small, medium, and large deciduous trees and the conifer. Releases of CO_2 associated with tree care activities account for less than 5 percent of net CO_2 sequestration.

Air quality improvement—

Air quality benefits are defined as the sum of pollutant uptake by trees and avoided power plant emissions owing to energy savings minus biogenic volatile organic compounds (BVOCs) released by trees. Average annual air quality benefits range from $3 to $13 per tree. The large-stature zelkova produced the greatest benefit because of its size and because it did not emit BVOCs. The average annual net benefit for eastern white pine was only $4 because of this species' high emissions of BVOCs (1 lb per year), which contribute to ozone formation. These high levels almost offset the air quality benefits from uptake of other pollutants.

Annual air quality benefits are $3 to $13 per tree

The ability of trees to reduce particulates and nitrogen dioxides in the air has the highest monetary value. For example, the average annual monetary value for a zelkova tree is estimated to be $3.70 for particulates and $3.22 for nitrogen dioxides. The value of reducing sulfur dioxides and ozone is less, $2.97 and $2.50 per year for the zelkova.

Forty years after planting, the average annual monetary values of air quality improvement for a yard tree opposite a west wall are $5, $13, $21, and $8, respectively, for the small, medium, and large deciduous trees and the conifer.

Chapter 4. Estimating Benefits and Costs for Tree Planting Projects in Your Community

This chapter shows two ways that benefit-cost information presented in this guide can be used. The first hypothetical example demonstrates how to adjust values from the guide for local conditions when the goal is to estimate benefits and costs for a proposed tree planting project. The second example explains how to compare net benefits derived from planting different types of trees. The last section discusses actions communities can take to increase the cost-effectiveness of their tree programs.

Applying Benefit-Cost Data

Rodbell Falls City Example

The hypothetical city of Rodbell Falls is located in the Northeast region and has a population of 24,000. Most of its street trees were planted in the 1930s, with silver maple (see "Common and Scientific Names" section) and London planetrees as the dominant species. Currently, the tree canopy cover is sparse because most of the trees have died and not been replaced. Many of the remaining street trees are in declining health. The city hired an urban forester 2 years ago, and an active citizens' group, the Green Team, has formed (fig. 20).

Figure 20—The hypothetical Green Team is motivated to re-green their community by planting 1,000 trees in 5 years.

Initial discussions among the Green Team, local utilities, the urban forester, and other partners led to a proposed urban forestry program. The program intends to plant 1,000 trees in Rodbell Falls over a 5-year period. Trained volunteers will plant ¾- to 1-in trees in the following proportions: 70 percent large-maturing, 15 percent medium-maturing, and 5 percent small-maturing deciduous trees, and 10 percent conifers. The total cost for planting will be $160 per tree. One hundred trees will be planted in parks, and the remaining 900 trees will be planted along Main Street and other downtown streets.

The Rodbell Falls City Council has agreed to maintain the current funding level for management of existing trees. Also, they will advocate formation of a municipal tree district to raise funds for the proposed tree-planting project. A municipal tree district is similar in concept to a landscape assessment district, which receives revenues based on formulas that account for the services different customers receive. For example, the proximity of customers to greenspace in a landscape assessment district may determine how much they pay for upkeep. A municipal tree district might receive funding from air quality districts, stormwater management agencies, electric utilities, businesses, and residents in proportion to the value of future benefits these groups will receive from trees in terms of air quality, hydrology, energy, carbon dioxide (CO_2) reduction, and property value. Such a district would require voter approval of a special assessment that charges recipients for tree planting and maintenance costs in proportion to the tangible benefits they receive from the new trees. The council needs to know the amount of funding required for tree planting and maintenance, as well as how the benefits will be distributed over the 40-year life of the project.

The first step: determine tree planting numbers

As a first step, the Rodbell Falls city forester and Green Team decided to use the tables in appendix B to quantify total cumulative benefits and costs over 40 years for the proposed planting of 1,000 public trees—700 large, 150 medium, and 50 small deciduous trees and 100 conifers.

Before setting up a spreadsheet to calculate benefits and costs, the team considered which aspects of Rodbell Fall's urban and community forestry project differ from the regional values used in this guide (the methods for calculating the values in app. 2 are described in app. 3):

1. The prices of electricity and natural gas in Rodbell Falls are $0.11/kWh or $0.0125/kBtu, not $0.14/kWh or $0.0148/kBtu as assumed in this guide. It is assumed that the buildings that will be shaded by the new street trees have air conditioning and natural-gas heating.

2. The Green Team projected future annual costs for monitoring tree health and implementing their stewardship program. Administration costs are estimated to

average $2,500 annually for the life of the trees or $2.50 per tree each year. This guide assumed an average annual administration cost of between $3 and $7 per tree for large public trees. Thus, an adjustment is necessary.

3. Planting will cost $300 per tree. The guide assumes planting costs of $400 per public tree. The costs will be slightly lower for Rodbell Falls because labor will be provided by trained volunteers.

To calculate the dollar value of total benefits and costs for the 40-year period, the forester created a spreadsheet table (table 4). Each benefit and cost category is listed in the first column. Prices, some adjusted for Rodbell Falls where necessary, are entered into the second column. The third column contains the *resource units* (RU) per tree per year associated with the benefit or the cost per tree per year, which can be found in appendix 2. For aesthetic and other benefits, the dollar values for public trees are placed in the RU columns. The fourth column lists the 40-year total values, obtained by multiplying the RU values by tree numbers, prices, and 40 years.

The second step: adjust for local prices of benefits

To adjust for different electricity prices, the forester multiplied electricity saved for a large public tree in the RU column (88.3 kWh) by the Rodbell Falls price for electricity ($0.11/kWh). This value ($9.71 per tree per year) was then multiplied by the number of trees planted and 40 years ($9.71 × 700 trees × 40 years = $271,841) to obtain cumulative air-conditioning energy savings for the large public trees (table 4). The process was carried out for all benefits and all tree types.

The third step: adjust for local costs

To adjust cost figures, the city forester changed the planting cost from $400 assumed in the guide to $300 (table 4). This planting cost was annualized by dividing the cost per tree by 40 years ($300/40 = $7.50 per tree per year). Total planting costs were calculated by multiplying this value by 700 large trees and 40 years ($210,000).

The fourth step: calculate net benefits and benefit-cost ratios for public trees

The administration, inspection, and outreach costs are expected to average $2.50 per tree per year, or a total of $100 per tree for the project's life. Consequently, the total administration cost for large trees is $2.50 × 700 large trees × 40 years ($70,000). The same procedure was followed to calculate costs for the medium and small deciduous trees and conifers.

Subtracting total costs from total benefits yields net benefits:

- Small deciduous trees: $21,466 or $10.73 per tree per year

- Medium deciduous trees: $314,641 or $52.44 per tree per year

- Large deciduous trees: $3,116,047 over 40 years or $111.29 per tree per year

- Conifers: $128,093 or $32.02 per tree per year

Annual benefits over 40 years total $4.6 million ($114 per tree per year), and annual costs total a little less than $1 million ($24 per tree per year). The total net

Table 4—Spreadsheet calculations of benefits and costs for the Rodbell Falls plantin project (1,000 trees) over 40 years

Benefits	Adjusted price	50 small trees		150 medium trees		700 large trees		100 conifer trees		1,000 total trees		
		Resource units	Total value	Resource units	Total value	Resource units	Total value	Resource units	Total value	Total value	Per tree	Share of total benefits
	Dollars	*Resource units per tree per year*	*Dollars*	*Resource units per tree per year*	*Dollars*	*Resource units per tree per year*	*Dollars*	*Resource units per tree per year*	*Dollars*	*Dollars*	*Dollars per tree per year*	*Percent*
Electricity (kWh)	0.11	17	3,663	39	25,549	88.3	271,841	25	11,216	312,268	7.81	6.9
Natural gas (kBtu)	0.0125	829	20,725	1,567	117,525	2,913	1,019,550	1,547	77,350	1,235,150	30.88	27.1
Net carbon dioxide (lb)	0.0033	144	962	250	5,010	485	45,357	218	2,912	54,242	1.36	1.2
Ozone (lb)	4.59	0.14	1,286	0.29	7,989	0.54	69,426	0.28	5,143	83,844	2.10	1.8
Nitrogen dioxide (lb)	4.59	0.18	1,652	0.37	10,190	0.70	89,964	0.34	6,242	108,049	2.70	2.4
Sulfur dioxide (lb)	3.48	0.15	1,044	0.40	8,356	0.85	82,860	0.23	3,203	95,463	2.39	2.1
Small particulate matter (lb)	8.31	0.13	2,160	0.33	16,450	0.45	104,684	0.37	12,296	135,591	3.39	3
Volatile organic compounds (lb)	2.31	0.01	46	0.03	417	0.06	3,889	0.02	185	4,537	0.11	0.1
Biogenic volatile organic compounds (lb)	2.31	0	0	-0.15	-2,083	0	0	-1.07	-9,908	-11,991	-0.30	-0.3
Hydrology (gal)	0.008	358	5,728	1,156	55,488	1,909	427,616	909	29,088	517,920	12.95	11.4
Aesthetics and other		8.03	16,060	32.84	197,040	61.93	1,734,040	17.13	68,520	2,015,660	50.39	44.3
Total benefits			53,327		441,930		3,849,227		206,248	4,550,731	113.77	100.0

Costs	50 small trees		150 medium trees		700 large trees		100 conifer trees		1,000 total trees		
	Per tree	Total value	Per tree	Total value	Per tree	Total value	Per tree	Total value	Per tree	Total value	Share of costs
	Dollars per tree per year	*Dollars*	*Dollars per tree per year*	*Dollars*	*Dollars per tree per year*	*Dollars*	*Dollars per tree per year*	*Dollars*	*Dollars per tree per year*	*Dollars*	*Percent*
Tree and planting	7.50	15,000	7.50	45,000	7.50	210,000	7.50	30,000	7.50	300,000	31
Pruning	3.26	6,525	7.69	46,169	11.60	324,863	6.40	25,583	10.08	403,139	42
Remove and dispose	1.28	2,563	1.62	9,744	2.06	57,634	1.47	5,873	1.90	75,813	8
Infrastructure repair	1.13	2,263	1.55	9,283	2.06	57,671	1.37	5,466	1.87	74,683	8
Cleanup	0.26	511	0.35	2,094	0.46	13,011	0.31	1,233	0.42	16,849	2
Liability and legal	0.00	0	0.00	0	0.00	0	0.00	0	0.00	0	0
Admin and other	2.50	5,000	2.50	15,000	2.50	70,000	2.50	10,000	2.50	100,000	10
Total costs		31,861		127,289		733,179		78,155	24.26	970,484	100
Net benefit		21,466		314,641		3,116,047		128,093	89.51	3,580,248	
Benefit/cost ratio		1.67		3.47		5.25		2.64		4.69	

annual benefits for all 1,000 trees over the 40-year period are $3.6 million, or $90 per tree. To calculate this average annual net benefit per tree, the forester divided the total net benefit by the number of trees planted (1,000) and 40 years ($3,580,248 / 1,000 trees / 40 years = $89.51). Dividing total benefits by total costs yielded benefit-cost ratios (BCRs) of 1.67, 3.47, 5.25 and 2.64 for small, medium, and large deciduous trees, and conifers, respectively. The BCR for the entire planting is 4.69, indicating that $4.69 will be returned for every $1 invested.

It is important to remember that this analysis assumes 34 percent of the planted trees die and does not account for the time value of money from a municipal capital investment perspective. Use the municipal discount rate to compare this investment in tree planting and management with alternative municipal investments.

The city forester and Green Team now know that the project will cost about $1 million, and the average annual cost will be $24,262 ($970,484 / 40 years); however, more funds will be needed initially for planting and stewardship.

The fifth and last step is to identify the distribution of functional benefits that the trees will provide. The last column in table 4 shows the distribution of positive benefits as a percentage of the total:

- Energy savings = 34 percent (cooling = 6.9 percent, heating = 27.1 percent)

- Carbon dioxide reduction = 1.2 percent

- Stormwater-runoff reduction = 11.4 percent

- Aesthetics/property value increase = 44.3 percent

- Air quality = 9.1 percent

The final step: determine how benefits are distributed, and link these to sources of revenue

With this information the planning team can determine how to distribute the costs for tree planting and maintenance based on who benefits from the services the trees will provide. For example, assuming the goal is to generate enough annual revenue to cover the total costs of managing the trees ($1 million), fees could be distributed in the following manner:

Distributing costs of tree management to multiple parties

- $340,000 from electric and natural gas utilities for energy savings (34 percent). (It is more cost-effective for utility companies to plant trees to reduce peak energy demand than to meet peak needs through added infrastructure.)

- $12,000 from local industry for atmospheric CO_2 reductions (1.2 percent).

- $114,000 from the stormwater-management district for water quality improvement associated with reduced runoff (11.4 percent).

- $443,000 from property owners for increased property values (44.3 percent).

- $91,000 from air quality management district for net reduction in air pollutants (9.1 percent).

Whether project funds are sought from partners, the general fund, or other sources, this information can assist managers in developing policy, setting priorities, and making decisions. The Center for Urban Forest Research has developed a computer program called STRATUM, part of the i-Tree software suite, that simplifies these calculations for analysis of existing street tree populations (Maco and McPherson 2003; http://www.itreetools.org).

City of Buscainoville Example

As a municipal cost-cutting measure, the hypothetical city of Buscainoville plans to stop planting street trees in areas of new development. Instead, developers will be required to plant front yard trees, thereby reducing costs to the city. The community forester and concerned citizens believe that, although this policy will result in lower planting costs for the city, developers may plant trees with smaller mature size than the city would have. Currently, Buscainoville's policy is to plant large-growing trees based on each site's available growing space (fig. 21). Planting smaller-stature trees could result in benefits "forgone" that will exceed cost savings. To evaluate this possible outcome, the community forester and concerned citizens decided to compare costs and benefits of planting small, medium, and large trees for a hypothetical street-tree planting project in Buscainoville.

The first step: calculate benefits and costs over 40 years

As a first step, the city forester and concerned citizens decided to quantify the total cumulative benefits and costs over 40 years for a typical street tree planting of 1,500 trees in Buscainoville. For comparison purposes, the planting includes 500 small trees, 500 medium trees,

Figure 21—The policy of the fictional city of Buscainoville's policy to plant as large a tree as the site will handle has provided ample benefits in the past. Here, large-stature trees have been planted

and 500 large trees. Data in appendix 2 are used for the calculations; however, three aspects of Buscainoville's urban and community forestry program are different than assumed in this tree guide:

1. The price of electricity is $0.17/kWh, not $0.14/kWh.

2. The trees will be irrigated for the first 5 years at a cost of approximately $0.50 per tree annually.

3. Planting costs are $450 per tree for city trees instead of the $400 per tree.

To calculate the dollar value of total benefits and costs for the 40-year period, the last column in appendix 2 (40-year average) is multiplied by 40 years. As this value is for one tree, it must be multiplied by the total number of trees planted in the respective small, medium, or large tree size classes. To adjust for higher electricity prices, we multiply electricity saved for each tree type in the RU column by the number of trees and 40 years (large tree: 88 kWh × 500 trees × 40 years = 1,760,000 kWh). This value is multiplied by the price of electricity in Buscainoville ($0.17/kWh × 1,760,000 kWh = $299,200) to obtain cumulative air-conditioning energy savings for the 500 large trees (table 5).

The second step: adjust for local prices of benefits

All the benefits are summed for each size tree for a 40-year period. The 500 small trees provide $554,819 in total benefits. The medium and large trees provide $1.5 million and $2.9 million, respectively.

To adjust cost figures, we add a value for irrigation by multiplying the annual cost by the number of trees by the number of years irrigation will be applied ($0.50 × 500 trees × 5 years = $1,250). We multiply 500 trees by the unit planting cost ($450) to obtain the adjusted cost for planting in Buscainoville (500 × $450 = $225,000). The average annual 40-year costs taken from appendix 2 for other items are multiplied by 40 years and the appropriate number of trees to compute total costs. These 40-year cost values are entered into table 5.

The third step: adjust for local costs

Subtracting total costs from total benefits yields net benefits for the small ($130,769), medium ($961,650), and large ($2.16 million) trees. The total net benefit for the 40-year period is $3.3 million (total benefits − total costs), or $2,208 per tree ($3.3 million/1,500 trees) on average (table 5).

The net benefits per public tree planted are as follows:

- $262 for a small tree
- $1,923 for a medium tree
- $4,321 for a large tree

By not investing in street-tree planting, the city would save $675,000 in initial costs. There is a risk, however, that developers will not plant the largest

The fourth step: calculate cost savings and benefits foregone

trees possible. If the developer planted 1,500 small trees, benefits would total $1.7 million (3 × $554,819 for 500 small trees). If 1,500 large trees were planted, benefits would total $8.5 million. Planting all small trees would cost the city $6.8 million in forgone benefits. This amount far exceeds the savings of $675,000 obtained by requiring developers to plant new street trees, and suggests that, when turning over the responsibility for tree planting to others, the city should be very careful to develop and enforce a street tree ordinance that requires planting large trees where feasible.

Based on this analysis, the City of Buscainoville decided to retain the policy of promoting planting of large trees where space permits. They now require tree shade plans that show how developers will achieve 50 percent shade over streets, sidewalks, and parking lots within 15 years of development.

Table 5—Spreadsheet calculations of benefits and costs for the Buscainoville planting project (1,500 trees) over 40 years

Benefits	500 small		500 medium		500 large		1,500 tree total			
	Resource units	Total value	Resource units	Total value	Resource units	Total value	Resource units	Total value	Value per tree	Share of benefits
		Dollars		Dollars		Dollars		- - - - - Dollars - - - - -		Percent
Electricity (kWh)	340,000	57,800	780,000	132,600	1,760,000	299,200	2,880,000	489,600	326	9.8
Natural gas (kBtu)	16,580,000	207,200	31,340,000	391,800	58,260,000	728,200	106,180,000	1,327,200	885	26.6
Net carbon dioxide (lb)	2,880,000	9,619	5,000,000	16,700	9,700,000	32,398	17,580,000	58,717	78	2.4
Ozone (lb)	2,760	12,600	5,770	26,400	10,890	50,000	19,420	89,000	59	1.8
Nitrogen dioxide (lb)	3,540	16,200	7,410	34,000	14,040	64,400	24,990	114,600	76	2.3
Sulfur dioxide (lb)	3,090	10,800	8,000	27,800	17,040	59,400	28,130	98,000	65	2.0
Small particulate matter (lb)	2,670	22,200	6,600	54,800	8,910	74,000	18,180	151,000	101	3.0
Volatile organic compounds (lb)	260	600	630	1,400	1,300	3,000	2,190	5,000	3	0.1
Biogenic volatile organic compounds (lb)	-40	0	-2,960	-6,800	0	0	-3,000	-6,800	-5	-0.1
Hydrology (gal)	7,160,000	57,200	23,120,000	185,000	38,180,000	305,400	68,460,000	547,600	365	11.0
Aesthetics and other benefits		160,600		656,800		1,238,600		2,056,000	1,371	41.2
Total benefits		554,819		1,520,500		2,854,598		4,929,917	3,326	100.0

Costs		Total value		Total value		Total value		Total value	Value per tree	Share of costs
		Dollars		Dollars		Dollars		- - - - - Dollars - - - - -		Percent
Tree and planting		225,000		225,000		225,000		675,000	450	40.3
Pruning		65,200		153,800		232,000		451,000	301	26.9
Remove and dispose		25,600		32,400		41,200		99,200	66	5.9
Infrastructure		22,600		31,000		41,200		94,800	63	5.7
Irrigation		1,250		1,250		1,250		3,750	3	0.2
Cleanup		5,200		7,000		9,200		21,400	14	1.3
Liability and legal		0		0		0		0	0	0.0
Admin and other		79,200		108,400		144,200		331,800	221	19.8
Total costs		424,050		558,850		694,050		1,676,950	1,118	100.0
Net benefits		130,769		961,650		2,160,548		3,252,967	2,208	
Benefit / cost ratio		1.31		2.72		4.11		2.94		

This analysis assumed 34 percent of the planted trees died. It did not account for the time value of money from a capital investment perspective, but this could be done by using the municipal discount rate.

Increasing Program Cost-Effectiveness

What if the program you have designed is promising in terms of stormwater-runoff reduction, energy savings, volunteer participation, and additional benefits, but the costs are too high? This section describes some steps to consider that may increase benefits and reduce costs, thereby increasing cost-effectiveness.

What if costs are too high?

Increasing Benefits

Improved stewardship to increase the health and survival of recently planted trees is one strategy for increasing cost-effectiveness. An evaluation of the Sacramento Shade program found that tree survival rates had a substantial impact on projected benefits (Hildebrandt et al. 1996). Higher survival rates increase energy savings and reduce tree removal and planting costs.

Work to increase survival rates

Conifers and broadleaf evergreens intercept rainfall and particulate matter year round as well as reduce windspeeds and provide shade, which lowers summer-cooling and winter-heating costs. Locating these types of trees in yards, parks, school grounds, and other open-space areas can increase benefits.

Target tree plantings with highest return

You can further increase energy benefits by planting a higher percentage of trees in locations that produce the greatest energy savings, such as opposite west-facing walls and close to buildings with air conditioning. Keep in mind that evergreen trees should not be planted on the southern side of buildings, because their branches and leaves block the warm rays of the winter sun. By customizing tree locations to increase numbers in high-yield sites, energy savings can be boosted.

Customize planting locations

Reducing Program Costs

Cost effectiveness is influenced by program costs as well as benefits:

Cost effectiveness = Total benefit / total program cost

Cutting costs is one strategy to increase cost effectiveness. A substantial percentage of total program costs occur during the first 5 years and are associated with tree planting and establishment (McPherson 1993). Some strategies to reduce these costs include:

Reduce up-front and establishment costs

- Plant bare-root or smaller tree stock.
- Use trained volunteers for planting and pruning of young trees (fig. 22).
- Provide followup care to increase tree survival and reduce replacement costs.
- Select and locate trees to avoid conflicts with infrastructure.

Use less expensive stock where appropriate

Where growing conditions are likely to be favorable, such as yard or garden settings, it may be cost-effective to use smaller, less expensive stock or bare-root trees. In highly urbanized settings and sites subject to vandalism, however, large stock may survive the initial establishment period better than small stock.

Investing in the resources needed to promote tree establishment during the first 5 years after planting is usually worthwhile, because once trees are established they have a high probability of continued survival. If your program has targeted trees on private property, then encourage residents to attend tree-care workshops. Develop standards of "establishment success" for different types of tree species. Perform periodic inspections to alert residents to tree health problems, and reward those whose trees meet your program's establishment standards. Replace dead trees as soon as possible, and identify ways to improve survivability.

Although organizing and training volunteers requires labor and resources, it is usually less costly than contracting the work. A cadre of trained volunteers can easily maintain trees until they reach a height of about 20 ft and limbs are too high to prune from the ground with pole pruners. By the time trees reach this size, they are well established. Pruning during this establishment period should result in trees that will require less care in the long term. Training young trees can provide

Figure 22—Trained volunteers can plant and maintain young trees, allowing the community to accomplish more at less cost and providing satisfaction for participants (photo courtesy of Tree Trust).

a strong branching structure that requires less frequent thinning and shaping (Costello 2000). Ideally, young trees should be inspected and pruned every other year for the first 5 years after planting.

Prune early

As trees grow larger, pruning costs may increase on a per-tree basis. The frequency of pruning will influence these costs, as it takes longer to prune a tree that has not been pruned in 10 years than one that was pruned a few years ago. Although pruning frequency varies by species and location, a return frequency of about 5 to 8 years is usually sufficient for older trees (Miller 1997).

Carefully select and locate trees to avoid conflicts with overhead power lines, sidewalks, and underground utilities. Time spent planning the planting will result in long-term savings. Also consider soil type and irrigation, microclimate, and the type of activities occurring around the tree that will influence its growth and management.

Match tree to site

When evaluating the bottom line—trees pay us back—do not forget to consider benefits other than the stormwater-runoff reductions, energy savings, atmospheric CO_2 reductions, and other tangible benefits. The magnitude of benefits related to employment opportunities, job training, community building, reduced violence, and enhanced human health and well-being can be substantial (fig. 23). Moreover, these benefits extend beyond the site where trees are planted, furthering collaborative efforts to build better communities.

**It all adds up—
trees pay us back**

For more information on urban and community forestry program design and implementation, see the list of additional resources in appendix 1.

Figure 23—Trees pay us back in tangible and intangible ways (photo courtesy of Phillip Rodbell).

Chapter 5. General Guidelines for Selecting and Placing Trees

In this chapter, general guidelines for selecting and locating trees are presented. Residential trees and trees in public places are considered.

Guidelines for Energy Savings

Maximizing Energy Savings From Shading

Where should shade trees be planted?

The right tree in the right place can save energy and reduce tree care costs. In midsummer, the sun shines on the east side of a building in the morning, passes over the roof near midday, and then shines on the west side in the afternoon (fig. 4). Electricity use is highest during the afternoon when temperatures are warmest and incoming sunshine is greatest. Therefore, the west side of a home is the most important side to shade (Sand 1994).

Depending on building orientation and window placement, sun shining through windows can heat a home quickly during the morning hours. The east side is the second most important side to shade when considering the net impact of tree shade on energy savings (fig. 24). Deciduous trees on the east side provide summer shade and more winter solar heat gain than evergreens.

Figure 24—Locate trees to shade west and east windows (from Sand 1993).

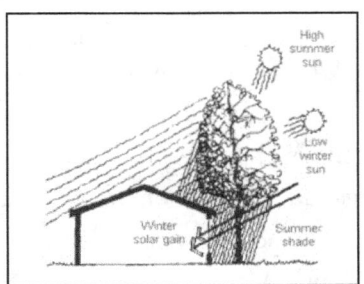

Figure 25—Select solar-friendly trees for southern exposures and locate them close enough to provide winter solar access and summer shade (from Sand 1991).

Trees located to shade south walls can block winter sunshine and increase heating costs because during winter the sun is lower in the sky and shines on the south side of homes (fig. 25). The warmth the sun provides is an asset, so do not plant evergreen trees that will block southern exposures and solar collectors. Use **solar-friendly trees** to the south because the bare branches of these deciduous trees allow most sunlight to strike the building (some solar-unfriendly deciduous trees can reduce sunlight striking the south side of buildings by 50 percent even without leaves) (Ames 1987). Examples of solar-friendly trees include most species and

Figure 26—Trees south of a home before and after pruning. Lower branches are pruned up to increase heat gain from winter sun (from Sand 1993).

cultivars of maples, hackberry, honey locust, Kentucky coffeetree, and Japanese pagodatree (see "Common and Scientific Names" section). Some solar-unfriendly trees include most oaks, sycamore, most elms, basswood, river birch, and horse chestnut (McPherson et al. 1994).

To maximize summer shade and minimize winter shade, locate shade trees about 10 to 20 ft south of the home. As trees grow taller, prune lower branches to allow more sun to reach the building if this will not weaken the tree's structure (fig. 26).

The closer a tree is to a home the more shade it provides, but roots of trees that are too close can damage the foundation. Branches that impinge on the building can make it difficult to maintain exterior walls and windows. Keep trees 10 ft or farther from the home depending on mature crown spread, to avoid these conflicts. Trees within 30 to 50 ft of the home most effectively shade windows and walls.

Paved patios and driveways can become heat sinks that warm the home during the summer. Shade trees can make them cooler and more comfortable spaces. If a home is equipped with an air conditioner, shading can reduce its energy use, but do not plant vegetation so close that it will obstruct the flow of air around the unit.

Plant only small-growing trees under overhead power lines and avoid planting directly above underground water and sewer lines if possible. Contact your local utility location service before planting to determine where underground lines are located and which tree species should not be planted below power lines.

Planting Windbreaks for Heating Savings

A tree's size and crown density can make it ideal for blocking wind, thereby reducing the impacts of cold winter weather. Locate rows of trees perpendicular to the prevailing wind (fig. 27), usually the north and west sides of homes in the Northeast region.

Design the windbreak row to be longer than the building being sheltered because windspeed increases at the edge of the windbreak. Ideally, the windbreak should be planted upwind about 25 to 50 ft from the building and should consist of dense evergreens that will grow to twice the height of the building they shelter (Heisler 1986, Sand 1991). Avoid planting windbreaks that will block sunlight from south and east walls (fig. 28). Trees should be spaced close enough to form a dense screen, but not so close that they will block sunlight from each other, causing lower branches to self-prune. Most conifers can be spaced about 6 ft on center. If there is room for two or more rows, then space rows 10 to 12 ft apart.

Evergreens are preferred over deciduous trees for windbreaks because they provide better wind protection. The ideal windbreak tree is fast growing, visually dense, has strong branch attachments, and has stiff branches that do not self-prune. Large windbreak trees for communities in the Northeast include eastern white pine, Colorado spruce, and Norway spruce. Good windbreak species for smaller sites include eastern redcedar and arborvitae.

Plant dense evergreens

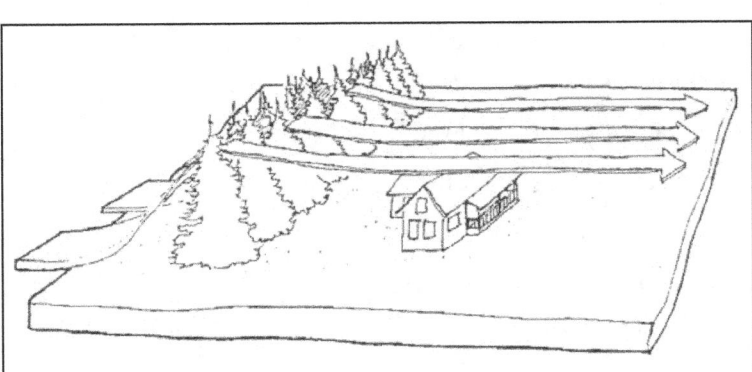

Figure 27—Evergreens protect a building from dust and cold by reducing windspeeds (from Sand 1993).

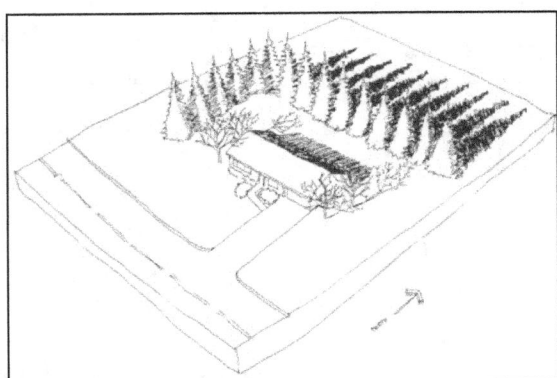

Figure 28—Midwinter shadows from a well-located windbreak and shade trees do not block solar radiation on the south-facing wall (from Sand 1993).

In settings where vegetation is not a fire hazard, evergreens planted close to the home create airspaces that reduce air infiltration and heat loss. Allow shrubs to form thick hedges, especially along north, west, and east walls.

Selecting Trees to Maximize Benefits

There are many choices

The ideal shade tree has a fairly dense, round crown with limbs broad enough to partially shade the roof. Given the same placement, a large tree will provide more shade than a small tree. Deciduous trees allow sun to shine through leafless branches in winter. Plant small trees where nearby buildings or power lines limit aboveground space. Columnar trees are appropriate in narrow side yards. Because the best location for shade trees is relatively close to the west and east sides of buildings, the most suitable trees will be strong and capable of resisting storm damage, disease, and pests (Sand 1994). Examples of trees not to select for placement near buildings include cottonwoods and silver maple because of their invasive roots, weak wood, and large size, and ginkgos because of their sparse shade and slow growth.

Picking the right tree

When selecting trees, match the tree's water requirements with those of surrounding plants. For instance, select low-water-use species for planting in areas that receive little irrigation. Also, match the tree's maintenance requirements with the amount of care and the type of use different areas in the landscape receive. For instance, tree species that drop fruit that can be a slip-and-fall problem should not be planted near paved areas that are frequently used by pedestrians. Check with your local landscape professional before selecting trees to make sure that they are well suited to the site's soil and climatic conditions.

Maximizing energy savings from trees

Use the following practices to plant and manage trees strategically to maximize energy conservation benefits:

- Increase community-wide tree canopy, and target shade to streets, parking lots, and other paved surfaces, as well as air-conditioned buildings.

- Shade west- and east-facing windows and walls.

- Avoid planting trees to the south of buildings.

- Select solar-friendly trees opposite east- and south-facing walls.

- Shade air conditioners, but don't obstruct airflow.

- Avoid planting trees too close to utilities and buildings.

- Create multirow, evergreen windbreaks where space permits, that are longer than the building.

Guidelines for Reducing Carbon Dioxide

Because trees in common areas and other public places may not shelter buildings from sun and wind and reduce energy use, carbon dioxide (CO_2) reductions are primarily due to sequestration. Fast-growing trees sequester more CO_2 initially than slow-growing trees, but this advantage can be lost if the fast-growing trees die at younger ages. Large trees have the capacity to store more CO_2 than smaller trees (fig. 29). To maximize CO_2 sequestration, select tree species that are well suited to the site where they will be planted. Consult with your local landscape professional or arborist to select the right tree for your site. Trees that are not well adapted will grow slowly, show symptoms of stress, or die at an early age. Unhealthy trees do little to reduce atmospheric CO_2 and can be unsightly liabilities in the landscape.

Design and management guidelines that can increase CO_2 reductions include the following:

- Maximize use of woody plants, especially trees, as they store more CO_2 than do herbaceous plants and grasses.

- Plant more trees where feasible and immediately replace dead trees to compensate for CO_2 lost through tree and stump removal.

Figure 29—Compared with small trees, large trees can store more carbon, filter more air pollutants, intercept more rainfall, and provide greater energy savings.

- Create a diverse assemblage of habitats, with trees of different ages and species, to promote a continuous canopy cover over time.

- Group species with similar landscape maintenance requirements together and consider how irrigation, pruning, fertilization, and efforts to control weeds, pests, and disease can be minimized.

- Reduce CO_2 associated with landscape management by using push mowers (not gas or electric), hand saws (not chain saws), pruners (not gas/electric shears), rakes (not leaf blowers), and employ landscape professionals who don't have to travel far to your site.

- Reduce maintenance by reducing turfgrass and planting drought-tolerant or environmentally friendly landscapes.

- Consider the project's lifespan when selecting species. Fast-growing species will sequester more CO_2 initially than slow-growing species but may not live as long.

- Provide ample space below ground for tree roots to grow so that they can maximize CO_2 sequestration and tree longevity.

- When trees die or are removed, salvage as much wood as possible for use as furniture and other long-lasting products to delay decomposition.

- Plant trees, shrubs, and vines in strategic locations to maximize summer shade and reduce winter shade, thereby reducing atmospheric CO_2 emissions associated with power production.

Guidelines for Reducing Stormwater Runoff

Trees are mini-reservoirs, controlling runoff at the source because their leaves and branch surfaces intercept and store rainfall, thereby reducing runoff volumes and erosion of watercourses, as well as delaying the onset of peak flows. Rainfall interception by large trees is a relatively inexpensive first line of defense in the battle to control nonpoint-source pollution.

When selecting trees to maximize rainfall interception benefits, consider the following:

- Select tree species with architectural features that maximize interception, such as large leaf surface area and rough surfaces that store water (Metro 2002).

- Increase interception by planting large trees where possible (fig. 30).

- Plant trees that are in leaf when precipitation is greatest.

- Select conifers because they have high interception rates, but avoid shading south-facing windows to maximize solar heat gain in winter.

- Plant low-water-use tree species where appropriate and native species that, once established, require little supplemental irrigation.

- In bioretention areas, such as roadside swales, select species that tolerate inundation, are long-lived, wide-spreading, and fast-growing (Metro 2002).

- Do not pave over streetside planting strips for easier weed control; this can reduce tree health and increase runoff.

Guidelines for Improving Air Quality Benefits

Trees, sometimes called the "lungs of our cities," are important because of their ability to remove contaminants from the air. The amount of gaseous pollutants and particulates removed by trees depends on their size and architecture, as well as local meteorology and pollutant concentrations.

Along streets, in parking lots, and in commercial areas, locate trees to maximize shade on paving and parked vehicles. Shade trees reduce heat that is stored or reflected by paved surfaces. By cooling streets and parking areas, trees reduce

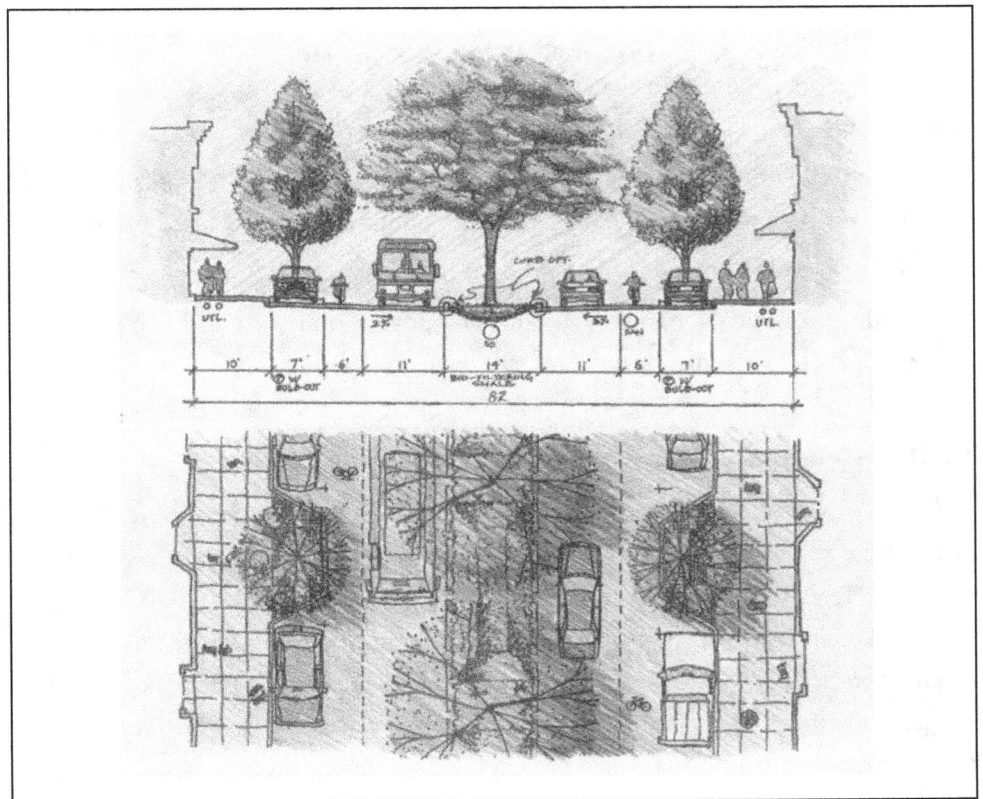

Figure 30—Trees can create a continuous canopy for maximum rainfall interception, even in commercial areas. In this example, a swale in the median filters runoff and provides ample space for large trees. Parking-space-sized planters contain the soil volume required to grow healthy, large trees (from Metro 2002).

emissions of evaporative hydrocarbons from parked cars and thereby reduce smog formation (Scott et al. 1999). Large trees can shade a greater area than smaller trees, but should be used only where space permits. Remember that a tree needs space for both branches and roots.

Tree planting and management guidelines to improve air quality include the following (Nowak 2000, Smith and Dochinger 1976):

- Select species that tolerate pollutants that are present in harmful concentrations. For example, in areas with high ozone concentration, avoid sensitive species such as white and green ash, tulip poplar, and Austrian pine (Noble et al. 1988).

- Conifers have high surface-to-volume ratios and retain their foliage year round, which may make them more effective than deciduous species.

- Species with long leaf stems (e.g., ash, maple) and hairy plant parts (e.g., oak, birch, sumac) are especially efficient interceptors.

- Effective uptake depends on proximity to the pollutant source and the amount of biomass. Where space permits, plant multilayered stands near the source of pollutants.

- Consider the local meteorology and topography to promote airflow that can "flush" pollutants out of the city along streets and greenspace corridors. Use columnar-shaped trees instead of spreading forms to avoid trapping pollutants under the canopy and obstructing airflow.

- In areas with unhealthy ozone concentrations, maximize use of plants that emit low levels of biogenic volatile organic compounds to reduce ozone formation.

- Sustain large, healthy trees; they produce the most benefits.

- To reduce emissions of volatile organic compounds and other pollutants, plant trees to shade parked cars and conserve energy.

Avoiding Tree Conflicts With Infrastructure

Conflicts between trees and infrastructure create lose-lose situations. Examples include trees growing into power lines, blocking traffic signs, and roots heaving sidewalks. Trees lose because often they must be altered or removed to rectify the problem. People lose directly because of the additional expense incurred to eliminate the conflict. They lose indirectly owing to benefits foregone when a large tree is replaced with a smaller tree, or too frequently, no tree at all. Tree conflicts with infrastructure are usually avoidable with good planning and judicious tree selection.

- Before planting, contact your local before-digging company, such as One-Call Center, Inc., or Miss Utility, to locate underground water, sewer, gas, and telecommunications lines.

- Avoid locating trees where they will block streetlights or views of traffic and commercial signs.

- Check with local transportation officials for sight visibility requirements. Keep trees at least 30 ft away from street intersections to ensure visibility.

- Avoid planting shallow-rooting species near sidewalks, curbs, and paving. Tree roots can heave pavement if planted too close to sidewalks and patios. Generally, avoid planting within 3 ft of pavement, and remember that trunk flare at the base of large trees can displace soil and paving for a considerable distance. Use strategies to reduce infrastructure damage by tree roots, such as meandering sidewalks around trees and ramping sidewalks over tree roots (Costello and Jones 2003).

- Select only small trees (<25 ft tall) for location under overhead power lines, and do not plant directly above underground water and sewer lines (fig. 31). Avoid locating trees where they will block illumination from streetlights or views of street signs in parking lots, commercial areas, and along streets.

For trees to deliver benefits over the long term, they require enough soil volume to grow and remain healthy. Matching tree species to the site's soil volume can reduce sidewalk and curb damage as well. Figure 32 shows recommended soil volumes for different sized trees.

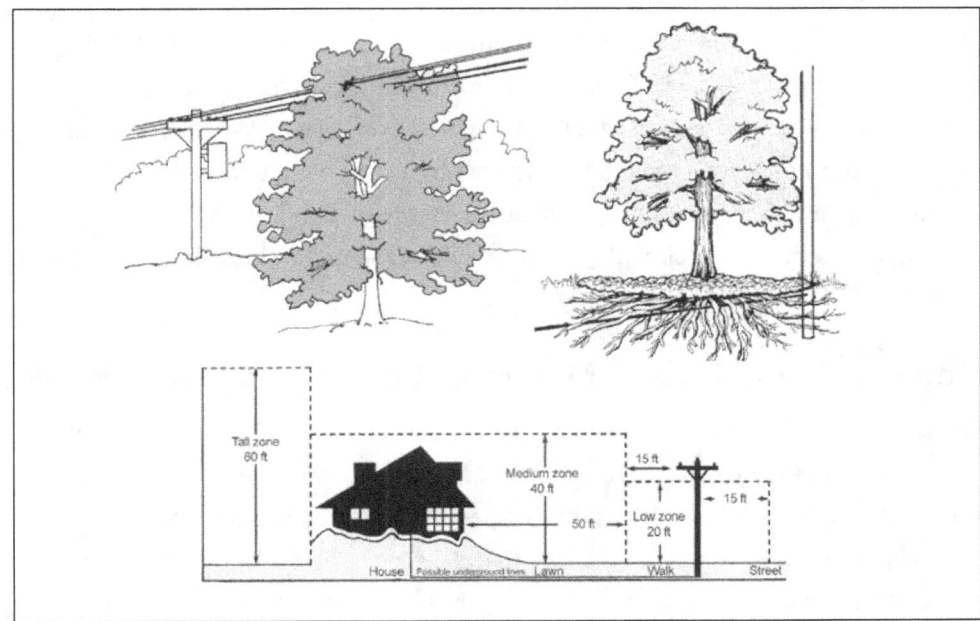

Figure 31—Know where power lines and other utility lines are before planting. Under power lines use only small-growing trees ("low zone"), and avoid planting directly above underground utilities. Larger trees may be planted where space permits ("medium" and "tall zones") (from ISA 1992).

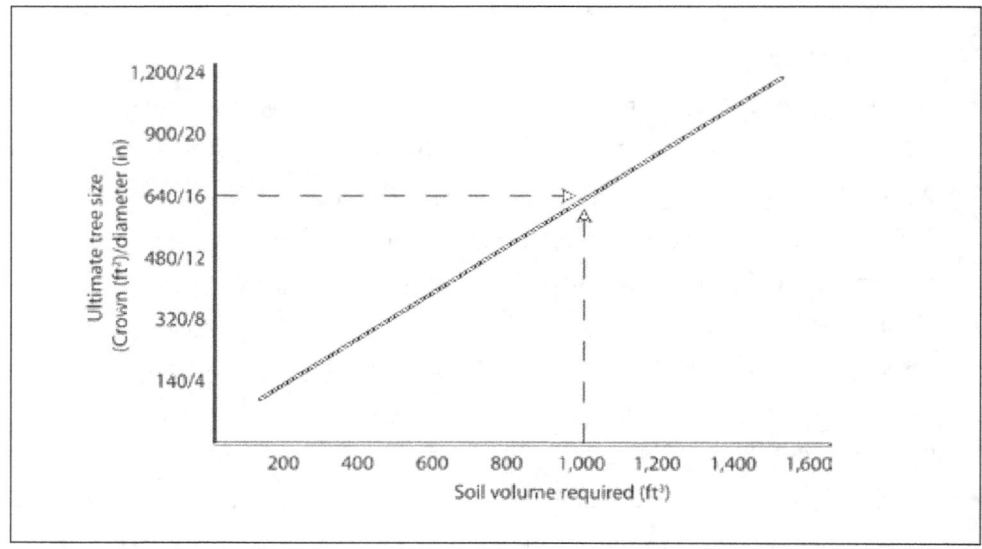

Figure 32—Developed from several sources by Urban (1992), this graph shows the relationship between tree size and required soil volume. For example, a tree with a 16-in diameter at breast height (41 cm) with 640 ft^2 of crown projection area (59.5 m^2 under the dripline) requires 1,000 ft^3 (28 m^3) of soil (from Costello and Jones 2003).

Maintenance requirements and public safety issues influence the types of trees selected for public places. The ideal public tree is not susceptible to wind damage and branch drop, does not require frequent pruning, produces negligible litter, is deep-rooted, has few serious pest and disease problems, and tolerates a wide range of soil conditions, irrigation regimes, and air pollutants. Because relatively few trees have all these traits, it is important to match the tree species to the planting site by determining what issues are most important on a case-by-case basis. For example, parking-lot trees should be tolerant of hot, dry conditions, have strong branch attachments, and be resistant to attacks by pests that leave vehicles covered with sticky exudates. Check with your local landscape professional for horticultural information on tree traits.

General Guidelines to Maximize Long-Term Benefits

Selecting a tree from the nursery that has a high probability of becoming a healthy, trouble-free **mature tree** is critical to a successful outcome. Therefore, select the very best stock at your nursery, and when necessary, reject nursery stock that does not meet industry standards. Make sure that the species you select is adapted to the site's growing conditions and is architecturally suited to the purpose at hand.

The health of the tree's root ball is critical to its ultimate survival. If the tree is in a container, check for matted roots by sliding off the container. Roots should penetrate to the edge of the root ball, but not densely circle the inside of the container or grow through drain holes. As well, at least two large structural roots should emerge from the trunk within 1 to 3 in of the soil surface. If there are no roots in the upper portion of the root ball, it is undersized or poorly formed and the tree should not be planted.

Another way to evaluate the quality of the tree before planting is to gently move the trunk back and forth. A good tree trunk bends and does not move in the soil, whereas a poor trunk bends a little and pivots at or below the soil line—a tell-tale sign of a poorly anchored tree. If the tree is balled and burlapped, be careful not to move the trunk too vigorously, as this could loosen the roots.

Dig the planting hole 1 in shallower than the depth of the root ball to allow for some settling after watering. Make the hole two to three times as wide as the root ball and loosen the sides of the hole to make it easier for roots to penetrate. Place the tree so that the root flare is at the top of the soil. If the structural roots have grown properly as described above, the top of the root ball will be slightly higher (1 to 2 in) than the surrounding soil to allow for settling. Backfill with the native soil unless it is very rocky or sandy, in which case you may want to add composted organic matter such as peat moss or shredded bark (fig. 33).

Planting trees in urban plazas, commercial areas, and parking lots poses special challenges owing to limited soil volume and poor soil structure. Engineered soils and other soil volume expansion solutions can be placed under the hardscape to increase rooting space while meeting engineering requirements. For more information on engineered soils see *Reducing Infrastructure Damage by Tree Roots: A Compendium of Strategies* (Costello and Jones 2003).

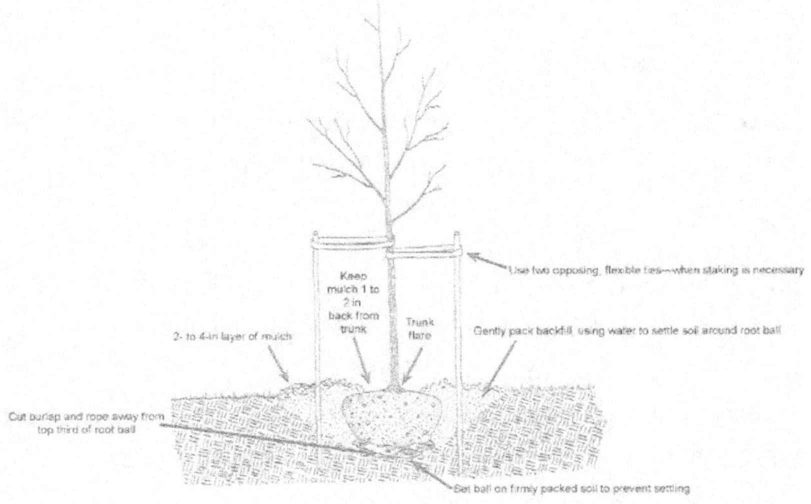

A good tree is well-anchored

Plant the tree in the right size hole

Figure 33—Prepare a broad planting area, plant the tree with the root flare at ground level, and provide a berm/water ring to retain water (drawing courtesy of International Society of Arboriculture).

Use the extra soil left after planting to build a berm outside the root ball that is 6 in high and 3 ft in diameter. Soak the tree, and gently rock it to settle it in. Handle only the ball so the trunk is not loosened. Cover the basin with a 2- to 4-in thick layer of mulch, but avoid placing mulch against the tree trunk. Water the new tree three times a week and increase the amount of water until the tree is established. Generally, a tree requires about 1 in of water per week. A rain gauge or soil moisture sensor (tensiometer) can help determine tree watering needs.

- Inspect your tree several times a year, and contact a local landscape professional if problems develop.

- If your tree needed staking to keep it upright, remove the stake and ties after 1 year or as soon as the tree can hold itself up. The staking should allow some tree movement, as this movement sends hormones to the roots causing them to grow and create greater tree stability. It also promotes trunk taper and growth.

- Reapply mulch and irrigate the tree as needed.

- Remove lower lateral branches after the first full year. Prune the young tree to maintain a central main trunk and equally spaced branches. For more information, see Costello (2000). As the tree matures, have it pruned by a certified arborist or other experienced professional to remove dead or damaged branches.

- By keeping your tree healthy, you maximize its ability to produce shade, intercept rainfall, reduce atmospheric CO_2, and provide other benefits.

For additional information on tree selection, planting, establishment, and care, see resources listed in appendix 1.

Glossary

AFUE—See annual fuel utilization efficiency.

annual fuel utilization efficiency (AFUE)—A measure of space-heating equipment efficiency defined as the fraction of energy output per energy input.

anthropogenic—Produced by humans.

avoided power plant emissions—Reduced emissions of carbon dioxide (CO_2) or other pollutants that result from reductions in building energy use owing to the moderating effect of trees on climate. Reduced energy use for heating and cooling results in reduced demand for electrical energy, which translates into fewer emissions by power plants.

biodiversity—The variety of life forms in a given area. Diversity can be categorized in terms of the number of species, the variety in the area's plant and animal communities, the genetic variability of the animals or plants, or a combination of these elements.

biogenic—Produced by living organisms.

biogenic volatile organic compounds (BVOCs)—Hydrocarbon compounds from vegetation (e.g., isoprene, monoterpene) that exist in the ambient air and contribute to the formation of smog or may themselves be toxic. Emission rates (μg/g/hr) used for this report follow Benjamin and Winer (1998):

Kwanzan cherry—0.0 (isoprene); 0.1 (monoterpene)

red maple—0.0 (isoprene); 2.8 (monoterpene)

Japanese zelkova— 0.0 (isoprene); 0.0 (monoterpene)

eastern white pine—0.0 (isoprene); 3.5 (monoterpene)

canopy—A layer or multiple layers of branches and foliage at the top or crown of a forest's trees.

canopy cover—The area of land surface that is covered by tree canopy, as seen from above.

Ccf—One hundred cubic feet.

climate—The average weather for a particular region and period (usually 30 years). Weather describes the short-term state of the atmosphere; climate is the average pattern of weather for a particular region. Climatic elements include precipitation, temperature, humidity, sunshine, wind velocity, phenomena such as fog, frost, and hailstorms, and other measures of weather.

climate effects—Impact on residential space heating and cooling (lb CO_2/tree per year) from trees located more than 50 ft (15 m) from a building owing to associated reductions in windspeeds and summer air temperatures.

community forests—The sum of all woody and associated vegetation in and around human settlements, ranging from small rural villages to metropolitan regions.

contract rate—The percentage of residential trees cared for by commercial arborists; the proportion of trees contracted out for a specific service (e.g., pruning or pest management).

control costs—The marginal cost of reducing air pollutants when using best available control technologies.

crown—The branches and foliage at the top of a tree.

cultivar (derived from "cultivated variety")—Denotes certain cultivated plants that are clearly distinguishable from others by any characteristic, and that when reproduced (sexually or asexually), retain their distinguishing characteristics. In the United States, "variety" is often considered synonymous with "cultivar."

deciduous—Trees or shrubs that lose their leaves every fall.

diameter at breast height (d.b.h.)—The diameter of a tree outside the bark measured 4.5 ft (1.37 m) above the ground on the uphill side (where applicable) of the tree.

dripline—The area beneath a tree marked by the outer edges of the branches.

emission factor—The rate of CO_2, NO_2, SO_2, and PM_{10} output resulting from the consumption of electricity, natural gas, or any other fuel source.

evapotranspiration (ET)—The total loss of water by evaporation from the soil surface and by transpiration from plants, from a given area, and during a specified period.

evergreens—Trees or shrubs that are never entirely leafless. Evergreens may be broadleaved or coniferous (cone-bearing with needlelike leaves).

greenspace—Urban trees, forests, and associated vegetation in and around human settlements, ranging from small communities in rural settings to metropolitan regions.

hardscape—Paving and other impervious ground surfaces that reduce infiltration of water into the soil.

heat sinks—Paving, buildings, and other surfaces that store heat energy from the sun.

hourly pollutant dry deposition—Removal of gases from the atmosphere by direct transfer to natural surfaces and absorption of gases and particles by natural surfaces such as vegetation, soil, water, or snow.

interception—Rainfall held on tree leaves and stem surfaces.

kBtu—A unit of work or energy, measured as 1,000 British thermal units. One kBtu is equivalent to 0.293 kWh.

kilowatt-hour (kWh)—A unit of work or energy, measured as 1 kW (1,000 watts) of power expended for 1 hour. One kWh is equivalent to 3.412 kBtu.

leaf area index (LAI)—Total leaf area per unit area of crown if crown were projected in two dimensions.

leaf surface area (LSA)—Measurement of area of one side of a leaf or leaves.

mature tree—A tree that has reached a desired size or age for its intended use. Size, age, and economic maturity differ depending on the species, location, growing conditions, and intended use.

mature tree size—The approximate size of a tree 40 years after planting.

MBtu—A unit of work or energy, measured as 1,000,000 British thermal units. One MBtu is equivalent to 0.293 MWh.

megawatt-hour (MWh)—A unit of work or energy, measured as 1 Megawatt (1,000,000 watts) of power expended for 1 hour. One MWh is equivalent to 3.412 MBtu.

metric tonne (t)—A measure of weight equal to 1,000,000 grams (1000 kg) or 2,205 pounds.

municipal forester—A person who manages public street and/or park trees (municipal forestry programs) for the benefit of the community.

nitrogen oxides (oxides of nitrogen, NOx)—A general term for compounds of nitric acid (NO), nitrogen dioxide (NO_2), and other oxides of nitrogen. Nitrogen oxides are typically created during combustion processes and are major contributors to smog formation and acid deposition. NO_2 may cause numerous adverse human health effects.

NO_2—See nitrogen oxides.

O_3—See ozone.

ozone (O_3)—A strong-smelling, pale blue, reactive toxic chemical gas with molecules of three oxygen atoms. It is a product of the photochemical process involving the Sun's energy. Ozone exists in the upper layer of the atmosphere as well as at the Earth's surface. Ozone at the Earth's surface can cause numerous adverse human health effects. It is a major component of smog.

peak flow (or peak runoff)—The maximum rate of runoff at a given point or from a given area, during a specific period.

photosynthesis—The process in green plants of converting water and CO_2 into sugar by using light energy; accompanied by the production of oxygen.

PM_{10} (particulate matter)—Major class of air pollutants consisting of tiny solid or liquid particles of soot, dust, smoke, fumes, and mists. The size of the particles (10 microns or smaller, about 0.0004 in or less) allows them to enter the air sacs (gas-exchange region) deep in the lungs where they may be deposited and cause adverse health effects. PM_{10} also reduces visibility.

resource unit (RU)—The value used to determine and calculate benefits and costs of individual trees. For example, the amount of air conditioning energy saved in kWh/year per tree, air-pollutant uptake in pounds/year per tree, or rainfall intercepted in gallons/year per tree.

riparian habitats—Narrow strips of land bordering creeks, rivers, lakes, or other bodies of water.

seasonal energy efficiency ratio (SEER)—Ratio of cooling output to power consumption; kBtu-output/kWh-input as a fraction. It is the Btu of cooling output during normal annual usage divided by the total electric energy input in kilowatt-hours during the same period.

sequestration—Removal of CO_2 from the atmosphere by trees through the processes of photosynthesis and respiration (lb CO_2/tree per year).

shade coefficient—The percentage of light striking a tree crown that is transmitted through gaps in the crown. This is the percentage of light that hits the ground.

shade effects—Impact on residential space heating and cooling (lb CO_2/tree per year) from trees located within 50 ft (15 m) of a building.

SO_2—See sulfur dioxide.

solar-friendly trees—Trees that have characteristics that reduce blocking of winter sunlight. According to one numerical ranking system, these traits include open crowns during the winter heating season, leaves that fall early and appear late, relatively small size, and a slow growth rate (Ames 1987).

stem flow—Rainfall that travels down the tree trunk and onto the ground.

sulfur dioxide (SO_2)—A strong-smelling, colorless gas that is formed by the combustion of fossil fuels. Power plants, which may use coal or oil high in sulfur content, can be major sources of SO_2. Sulfur oxides contribute to the problem of acid deposition.

t—See metric tonne.

therm—A unit of heat equal to 100,000 BTUs or 100 kBtu. Also, 1 kBtu is equal to 0.01 therm.

throughfall—Amount of rainfall that falls directly to the ground below the tree crown or drips onto the ground from branches and leaves.

transpiration—The loss of water vapor through the stomata of leaves.

tree or canopy cover—Within a specific area, the percentage covered by the crown of an individual tree or delimited by the vertical projection of its outermost perimeter; small openings in the crown are ignored. Used to express the relative importance of individual species within a vegetation community or to express the coverage of woody species.

tree litter—Fruit, leaves, twigs, and other debris shed by trees.

tree-related emissions—Carbon dioxide released when growing, planting, and caring for trees.

tree surface saturation storage capacity—The maximum volume of water that can be stored on a tree's leaves, stems, and bark. This part of rainfall stored on the canopy surface does not contribute to surface runoff during and after a rainfall event.

urban heat island—An area in a city where summertime air temperatures are 3 to 8 °F warmer than temperatures in the surrounding countryside. Urban areas are warmer for two reasons: (1) dark construction materials for roofs and asphalt absorb solar energy, and (2) few trees, shrubs, or other vegetation provide shade and cool the air.

volatile organic compounds (VOCs)—Hydrocarbon compounds that exist in the ambient air. VOCs contribute to the formation of smog or are themselves toxic. VOCs often have an odor. Some examples of VOCs are gasoline, alcohol, and the solvents used in paints.

willingness to pay—The maximum amount of money an individual would be willing to pay, rather than do without nonmarket, public goods and services provided by environmental amenities such as trees and forests.

Common and Scientific Names

Common name	Scientific name
Plants	
American basswood	*Tilia americana* L.
Arborvitae	*Thuja occidentalis* L.
Austrian pine	*Pinus nigra* J.F. Arnold
Birch	*Betula* spp.
Blackgum	*Nyssa* spp.
Colorado spruce	*Picea pungens* Engelm.
Cottonwood	*Populus* spp.
Eastern redcedar	*Juniperus virginiana* L.
Eastern white pine	*Pinus strobus* L.
Elms	*Ulmus* spp.
Gingko	*Ginkgo biloba* L.
Green ash	*Fraxinus pennsylvanica* Marshall
Hackberry	*Celtis occidentalis* L.
Hackberry	*Celtis* spp.
Honeylocust	*Gleditsia triacanthos* L.
Horse chestnut	*Aesculus hippocastanum* L.
Japanese pagodatree	*Styphnolobium japonica* (L.) Schott
Japanese zelkova	*Zelkova serrata* (Thunb.) Makino
Kentucky coffeetree	*Gymnocladus dioicus* (L.) K. Koch
Kwanzan cherry	*Prunus serrulata* 'Kwanzan' Lindl.
London planetree	*Platanus hybrida* Brot.
Maple	*Acer* spp.
Norway spruce	*Picea abies* (L.) Karst.
Oak	*Quercus* spp.
Poplar	*Populus* spp.
Red maple	*Acer rubrum* L.
Red oak	*Quercus rubra* L.
River birch	*Betula nigra* L.
Silver maple	*Acer saccharinum* L.
Sumac	*Rhus* spp.
Sweetgum	*Liquidambar styraciflua* L.
Sycamore	*Platanus* spp.
Tulip poplar	*Liriodendron tulipifera* L.
White ash	*Fraxinus americana* L.
White fir	*Abies concolor* (Gordon & Glend.) Lindl. ex Hildebr.

Insects

Asian long-horned beetle	*Anoplophora glabripennis* (Motschulsky)
Emerald ash borer	*Agrilus planipennis* Fairmaire

Pathogens

Dutch elm disease	*Ophiostoma ulmi* (Buisman) Nannf. and
	Ophiostoma novo-ulmi (Brasier)

Acknowledgments

We appreciate the technical assistance provided by Fiona Watt, Jacqueline Lu, Luke D'Orazio, Bram Gunther, Jennifer Greenfeld, Doreen Whitley, Brian Dugan, Adriana Jacykewycz, Joe Kocal, John Mueller, Mitchell Murdock, Laura Wooley, Joe Bonkowski, Arne Israel, Andrew Rabb, Bill Steyer, Rick Zeidler, and Daniel Arroyo (New York City Department of Parks and Recreation); Scott Maco, Jim Jenkins, and Jesse Hoekstra (Davey Resource Group); Brendan Buckley and John Sakulich (Tree Ring Laboratory, Lamont-Doherty Earth Observatory); Virginia Ambrose (US EPA); Keith Egleston (Northeast Regional Climate Center); Stephanie Huang, Christine Yang, and Aywon-Anh Nguyen (CUFR).

Tree care expenditure information was provided by Fiona Watt for New York City Department of Parks and Recreation, Ken Placko for Fairfield, Connecticut, Lon Hultgren for Mansfield, Connecticut, Dominique Agostino for Rocco Agostino Landscaping, Lloyd Allen for Ash Tree Service, and Dom D'Alonzo for Dom's Tree Service.

Fiona Watt (New York City Department of Parks and Recreation), Frank Dunstan (New York State Department of Environmental Conservation), and Gary Schwetz (Delaware Center for Horticulture) provided helpful reviews of this work.

Our thanks to Phillip Rodbell, Mark Buscaino, and Keith Cline (U.S. Department of Agriculture, Forest Service, State and Private Forestry), who provided invaluable support for this project. Tree ring aging was made possible with funds provided by the New York State Department of Environmental Conservation and the New York City Department of Parks and Recreation.

Metric Equivalents

When you know:	Multiply by:	To find:
Inches (in)	2.54	Centimeters (cm)
Feet (ft)	0.305	Meter (m)
Square feet (ft^2)	0.0929	Square meter (m^2)
Cubic feet (ft^3)	0.0283	Cubic meter (m^3)
Miles (mi)	1.61	Kilometers (km)
Square miles (mi^2)	2.59	Square kilometers (km^2)
Gallons (gal)	0.00378	Cubic meter (m^3)
Ounces	28.4	Grams (g)
Ounces	2.83×10^7	Micrograms or microns (μg)
Pounds (lb)	0.454	Kilogram (kg)
Pounds per square foot (lb/ft^2)	4.882	Kilograms per square meter (kg/m^2)
Tons (ton)	0.907	Metric tonne (t)
Thousand British thermal units (kBtu)	1.05	Megajoules (MJ)
Thousand British thermal units	0.293	Kilowatt-hours (kWh)
Degrees Fahrenheit (°F)	0.556(F - 32)	Degrees Celsius
Million British thermal units per hours	0.293	Megawatts (MW)

References

Akbari, H.; Davis, S.; Dorsano, S.; Huang, J.; Winnett, S., eds. 1992. Cooling our communities: a guidebook on tree planting and light-colored surfacing. Washington, DC: U.S. Environmental Protection Agency. 26 p.

Alliance for Community Trees. 2006. Tree by tree, street by street. http://actrees. org. (27 January 2007).

American Forests. 2002. Urban ecological analysis for the Washington, D.C. Metropolitan Area. Washington, DC. 16 p.

American Forests. 2003. Urban ecological analysis, Mecklenburg County, North Carolina. Washington, DC. 8 p.

American Forests. 2004. Urban ecological analysis, Montgomery, AL. Washington, DC. 12 p.

American Forests. 2006. Urban ecosystem analysis, Southeast Michigan and City of Detroit. Washington, DC. 15 p.

Ames, M.J. 1987. Solar friendly trees report. Portland, OR: City of Portland Energy Office. [Pages unknown].

Anderson, L.M.; Cordell, H.K. 1988. Residential property values improve by landscaping with trees. Southern Journal of Applied Forestry. 9: 162–166.

Bedker, P.J.; O'Brien, J.G.; Mielke, M.E. 1995. How to prune trees. NA-FR-01-95. Newtown Square, PA: U.S. Department of Agriculture, Forest Service, Northeastern Area State and Private Forestry. 28 p.

Bell, M.L.; McDermott, A.; Zeger, S.L.; Samet, J.M.; Dominici, F. 2004. Ozone and short-term mortality in 95 US urban communities. Journal of the American Medical Association. 292: 2372–2378.

Benjamin, M.T.; Winer, A.M. 1998. Estimating the ozone-forming potential of urban trees and shrubs. Atmospheric Environment. 32: 53–68.

Bernhardt, E.; Swiecki, T.J. 1993. The state of urban forestry in California: results of the 1992 California Urban Forest Survey. Sacramento: California Department of Forestry and Fire Protection. 51 p.

Bond, J. 2006. The Inclusion of large-scale tree planting in a state implementation plan. Geneva, NY: Davey Resource Group. 56 p.

Bratkovich, S.M. 2001. Utilizing municipal trees: ideas from across the country. NA-TP-06-01. Newtown Square, PA: U.S. Department of Agriculture, Forest Service, Northeastern Area State and Private Forestry. 91 p.

Brenzel, K.N., ed. 2001. Sunset Western garden book. 7th ed. Menlo Park, CA: Sunset Books, Inc. 768 p.

Cappiella, K.; Schueler, T.; Wright, T. 2005. Urban watershed forestry manual. Ellicot City, MD: Center for Watershed Protection. 138 p.

Cardelino, C.A.; Chameides, W.L. 1990. Natural hydrocarbons, urbanization, and urban ozone. Journal of Geophysical Research. 95(9): 13971–13979.

Chameides W.L.; Lindsay, R.W.; Richardson, J.; Kiang, C.S. 1988. The role of biogenic hydrocarbons in urban photochemical smog: Atlanta as a case study. Science. 241: 1473–1475.

Chicago Climate Exchange. 2007. About CCX. http://www.chicagoclimatex.com/about/index.html. (21 January 2007).

CO2e.com. 2007. CO$_2$e market size and pricing. http://www.co2e.com/strategies/AdditionalInfo.asp?PageID=273#1613. (21 January 2007).

Cohen, J.E.; Small, C.; Mellinger, A.; Gallup, J.; Sachs, J. 1997. Estimates of coastal populations. Science. 278(5341): 1211–1212.

ConEdison. 2006a. Residential and commercial energy prices. http://www.coned.com/documents/elec/201-210.pdf. (15 March 2006).

ConEdison. 2006b. Residential and commercial natural gas prices. http://www.coned.com/documents/gasrates.pdf. (15 March 2006).

Cook, D.I. 1978. Trees, solid barriers, and combinations: alternatives for noise control. In: Proceedings of the national urban forestry conference. ESF Pub. 80-003. Syracuse, NY: State University of New York: 330-334.

Costello, L.R. 2000. Training young trees for structure and form. [Video] V99-A. Oakland, CA: University of California, Agriculture and Natural Resources, Communication Services Cooperative Extension Service. 119 p.

Costello, L.R.; Jones, K.S. 2003. Reducing infrastructure damage by tree roots: a compendium of strategies. Cohasset, CA: Western Chapter of the International Society of Arboriculture. 119 p.

Costello, L.R.; Perry, E.J.; Matheny, N.P.; Henry, J.M.; Geisel, P.M. 2003. Abiotic disorders of landscape plants: a diagnostic guide. Publ. 3420. Oakland, CA: University of California Agriculture and Natural Resources. 242 p.

DeGaetano, A.T.; Eggleston, K.L.; Knapp, W.W. 1993. Daily solar radiation estimates for the Northeastern United States. NRCC Research Publication RR 93–4. Ithaca, NY: Northeast Regional Climate Center. 7 p.

Dwyer, J.F.; McPherson, E.G.; Schroeder, H.W.; Rowntree, R.A. 1992. Assessing the benefits and costs of the urban forest. Journal of Arboriculture. 18(5): 227–234.

Dwyer, M.C.; Miller, R.W. 1999. Using GIS to assess urban tree canopy benefits and surrounding greenspace distributions. Journal of Arboriculture. 25(2): 102–107.

Fazio, J.R. [N.d.]. Tree City USA Bulletin Series. Lincoln, NE: The National Arbor Day Foundation.

Gilman, E.F. 1997. Trees for urban and suburban planting. Albany, NY: Delmar Publishing. 688 p.

Gilman, E.F. 2002. An illustrated guide to pruning. 2nd ed. Albany, NY: Delmar Publishing. 256 p.

Gonzalez, S. 2004. Personal communication. Assistant maintenance superintendent, City of Vallejo, 111 Amador St., Vallejo, CA 94590.

Greeley, L.; Hansen, C. 2002. Combined sewer system long term control plan. Washington, DC: District of Columbia Water and Sewer Authority. [Pages unknown].

Grove, J.M.; O'Neil-Dunne, J.; Pelletier, K.; Nowak, D.; Walton, J. 2006. A report on New York City's present and possible urban tree canopy. South Burlington, VT: U.S. Department of Agriculture, Forest Service, Northeastern Research Station. [Pages unknown].

Guenther, A.B.; Monson, R.K.; Fall, R. 1991. Isoprene and monoterpene emission rate variability: observations with eucalyptus and emission rate algorithm development. Journal of Geophysical Research. 96: 10799–10808.

Guenther, A.B.; Zimmermann, P.R.; Harley, P.C.; Monson, R.K.; Fall, R. 1993. Isoprene and monoterpene emission rate variability: model evaluations and sensitivity analyses. Journal of Geophysical Research. 98: 12609–12617.

Hamburg, S.P.; Harris, N.; Jaeger, J.; Karl, T.R.; McFarland, M.; Mitchell, J.; Oppenheimer, M.; Santer, B.; Schneider, S.; Trenberth, K.; Wigley, T. 1997. Common questions about climate change. Nairobi, Kenya: United Nations Environment Programme, World Meteorological Organization. 22 p.

Hammer, T.T.; Coughlin, R.; Horn, E. 1974. The effect of a large urban park on real estate value. Journal of the American Institute of Planning. July: 274–275.

Hammond, J.; Zanetto, J.; Adams, C. 1980. Planning solar neighborhoods. Sacramento, CA: California Energy Commission. 179 p.

Hargrave, R.; Johnson, G.R.; Zins, M.E. 2002. Planting trees and shrubs for long-term health. MI-07681-S. St. Paul, MN: University of Minnesota Extension Service. 12 p.

Harris, R.W.; Clark, J.R.; Matheny, N.P. 2003. Arboriculture. 4th ed. Englewood Cliffs, NJ: Regents/Prentice Hall. 592 p.

Hauer, R.J.; Hruska, M.C.; Dawson, J.O. 1994. Trees and ice storms: the development of ice storm-resistant urban tree populations. Spec. Publ. 94-1. Urbana, IL: Department of Forestry, University of Illinois at Urbana-Champaign. 12 p.

Haugen, L.M. 1998. How to identify and manage Dutch elm disease. NA-PR-07-98. Newtown Square, PA: U.S. Department of Agriculture, Forest Service, Northeastern Area State and Private Forestry. 26 p.

Head, C.P.; Fisher, R.; O'Brien, M. 2001. Best management practices for community trees: a technical guide to tree conservation in Athens-Clarke County, Georgia. Athens, GA: Landscape Management Division Office. 134 p.

Heisler, G.M. 1986. Energy savings with trees. Journal of Arboriculture. 12(5): 113–125.

Hightshoe, G.L. 1988. Native trees, shrubs, and vines for urban and rural America. New York: Van Nostrand Reinhold. 832 p.

Hildebrandt, E.W.; Kallett, R.; Sarkovich, M.; Sequest, R. 1996. Maximizing the energy benefits of urban forestation. In: Proceedings of the ACEEE 1996 summer study on energy efficiency in buildings. Washington, DC: American Council for an Energy Efficient Economy: 121–131. Vol. 9.

Hudson, B. 1983. Private sector business analogies applied in urban forestry. Journal of Arboriculture. 9(10): 253–258.

Hull, R.B. 1992. How the public values urban forests. Journal of Arboriculture. 18(2): 98–101.

Intergovernmental Panel on Climate Change [IPCC]. 2001. Technical summary. Climate change 2001: the scientific basis. Geneva. 63 p.

International Society of Arboriculture [ISA]. 1992. Avoiding tree and utility conflicts. Savoy, IL. 4 p.

International Society of Arboriculture [ISA]. 2006. Welcome to the International Society of Arboriculture. http://www.isa-arbor.com/home.aspx. (27 January 2007).

Jo, H.K.; McPherson, E.G. 1995. Carbon storage and flux in urban residential green-space. Journal of Environmental Management. 45: 109–133.

Kaplan, R. 1992. Urban forestry and the workplace. In: Gobster, P.H., ed. Managing urban and high-use recreation settings. Gen. Tech. Rep. NC-163. St. Paul, MN: U.S. Department of Agriculture, Forest Service, North Central Research Station: 41–45.

Kaplan, R.; Kaplan, S. 1989. The experience of nature: a psychological perspective. Cambridge, United Kingdom: Cambridge University Press. 360 p.

Lewis, C.A. 1996. Green nature/human nature: the meaning of plants in our lives. Chicago, IL: University of Illinois Press. 176 p.

Lu, J. 2006. Personal communication. Urban Forester, Central Forestry and Horticulture, New York Department of Parks and Recreation, Olmsted Center, Flushing Meadow Corona Park, Flushing, NY 11368.

Luley, C.J.; Bond, J. 2002. A plan to integrate management of urban trees into air quality planning. Naples, NY: Davey Resource Group. 61 p.

Maco, S.E.; McPherson, E.G. 2003. A practical approach to assessing structure, function, and value of street tree populations in small communities. Journal of Arboriculture. 29(2): 84–97.

Marion, W.; Urban, K. 1995. User's manual for TMY2s—typical meteorological years. Golden, CO: National Renewable Energy Laboratory. 49 p.

Markwardt, L.J. 1930. Comparative strength properties of woods grown in the United States. Tech. Bull. 158. Washington, DC: U.S. Department of Agriculture. 38 p.

McHale, M. 2003. Carbon credit markets: Is there a role for community forestry? In: Kollin, C., ed. 2003 national urban forest conference proceedings. Washington, DC: American Forests: 74–77.

McPherson, E.G. 1984. Planting design for solar control. In: McPherson, E.G., ed. Energy-conserving site design. Washington, DC: American Society of Landscape Architects: 141–164. Chapter 8.

McPherson, E.G. 1992. Accounting for benefits and costs of urban greenspace. Landscape and Urban Planning. 22: 41–51.

McPherson, E.G. 1993. Evaluating the cost effectiveness of shade trees for demand-side management. The Electricity Journal. 6(9): 57–65.

McPherson, E.G. 1995. Net benefits of healthy and productive forests. In: Bradley, G.A., ed. Urban forest landscapes: integrating multidisciplinary perspectives. Seattle, WA: University of Washington Press: 180–194.

McPherson, E.G. 1997. Airing it out. Spring update. Davis, CA: U.S. Department of Agriculture, Forest Service, Pacific Southwest Research Station, Center for Urban Forest Research. 4 p.

McPherson, E.G. 1998. Atmospheric carbon dioxide reduction by Sacramento's urban forest. Journal of Arboriculture. 24(4): 215–223.

McPherson, E.G. 2000. Expenditures associated with conflicts between street tree root growth and hardscape in California. Journal of Arboriculture. 26(6): 289–297.

McPherson, E.G. 2001. Sacramento's parking lot shading ordinance: environmental and economic costs of compliance. Landscape and Urban Planning. 57: 105–123.

McPherson, E.G.; Mathis, S., eds. 1999. Proceedings of the Best of the West summit. Sacramento, CA: Western Chapter, International Society of Arboriculture. 93 p.

McPherson, E.G.; Muchnick, J. 2005. Effects of tree shade on asphalt concrete pavement performance. Journal of Arboriculture. 31(6): 303–309.

McPherson, E.G.; Peper, P.J. 1995. Infrastructure repair costs associated with street trees in 15 cities. In: Watson, G.W.; Neely, D., eds. Trees and building sites. Champaign, IL: International Society of Arboriculture: 49–63.

McPherson, E.G.; Nowak, D.J.; Heisler, G.; Grimmond, S.; Souch, C.; Grant, R.; Rowntree, R.A. 1997. Quantifying urban forest structure, function, and value: Chicago's Urban Forest Climate Project. Urban Ecosystems. 1: 49–61.

McPherson, E.G.; Nowak, D.J.; Rowntree, R.A. 1994. Chicago's urban forest ecosystem: results of the Chicago Urban Forest Climate Project. Gen. Tech. Rep. NE-186. Radnor [Newtown Square], PA: U.S. Department of Agriculture, Forest Service, Northeastern Research Station. 201 p.

McPherson, E.G.; Sacamano, P.L.; Wensman, S. 1993. Modeling benefits and costs of community tree plantings. Albany, CA: U.S. Department of Agriculture, Forest Service, Pacific Southwest Research Station. 170 p.

McPherson, E.G.; Simpson, J.R. 1999. Carbon dioxide reduction through urban forestry: guidelines for professional and volunteer tree planters. Gen. Tech. Rep. PSW-171. Albany, CA: U.S. Department of Agriculture, Forest Service, Pacific Southwest Research Station. 237 p.

McPherson, E.G.; Simpson, J.R. 2002. A comparison of municipal forest benefits and costs in Modesto and Santa Monica, CA, USA. Urban Forestry Urban Greening. 1: 61–74.

McPherson, E.G.; Simpson, J.R. 2003. Potential energy savings in buildings by an urban tree planting programme in California. Urban Forestry and Urban Greening. 2(2): 73–86.

McPherson, E.G.; Simpson, J.R.; Peper, P.J.; Gardner, S.L.; Vargas, K.E.; Maco, S.E.; Xiao, Q. 2006a. Piedmont community tree guide: benefits, costs, and strategic planting. Gen. Tech. Rep. PSW-GTR-200. Albany, CA: U.S. Department of Agriculture, Forest Service, Pacific Southwest Research Station. 95 p.

McPherson, E.G.; Simpson, J.R.; Peper, P.J.; Maco, S.E.; Gardner, S.L.; Cozad, S.K.; Xiao, Q. 2006b. Midwest community tree guide: benefits, costs, and strategic planting. Gen. Tech. Rep. PSW-GTR-199. Davis, CA: Albany, CA: U.S. Department of Agriculture, Forest Service, Pacific Southwest Research Station. 85 p.

McPherson, E.G.; Simpson, J.R.; Peper, P.J.; Xiao, Q. 1999. Tree guidelines for San Joaquin Valley communities. Sacramento, CA: Local Government Commission. 63 p.

Metro. 2002. Green streets: innovative solutions for stormwater and stream crossings. Portland, OR: Metro. 144 p.

Miller, R.W. 1997. Urban forestry: planning and managing urban greenspaces. 2nd ed. Upper Saddle River, NJ: Prentice-Hall. 502 p.

More, T.A.; Stevens, T.; Allen, P.G. 1988. Valuation of urban parks. Landscape and Urban Planning. 15: 139–152.

Morgan, R. 1993. A technical guide to urban and community forestry. Portland, OR: World Forestry Center.

Morgan, R. [N.d.]. An introductory guide to community and urban forestry in Washington, Oregon, and California. Portland, OR: World Forestry Center. 25 p.

National Arbor Day Foundation. 2006. Color your world. http://www.arborday. org. (27 January 2007).

Neely, D., ed. 1988. Valuation of landscape trees, shrubs, and other plants. 7th ed. Urbana, IL: International Society of Arboriculture. 50 p.

Noble, R.D.; Martin, J.L.; Jensen, K.F., eds. 1988. Air pollution effects on vegetation, including forest ecosystems. Proceedings of the second US–USSR symposium. Gov. Doc. A13.42/2:2:A:7. Broomall [Newtown Square], PA: U.S. Department of Agriculture, Forest Service, Northeastern Research Station. 311 p.

Nowak, D.J. 1994. Air pollution removal by Chicago's urban forest. In: McPherson, E.G.; Nowak, D.J.; Rowntree, R.A., eds. Chicago's urban forest ecosystem: results of the Chicago Urban Forest Climate Project. Gen. Tech. Rep. NE-186. Radnor [Newtown Square], PA: U.S. Department of Agriculture, Forest Service, Northeastern Research Station: 63–82.

Nowak, D.J. 2000. Tree species selection, design, and management to improve air quality. In: Scheu, D.L., ed. 2000 ASLA annual meeting proceedings. Washington, DC: American Society of Landscape Architects: 23–27.

Nowak, D.J.; Civerolo, K.L.; Rao, S.T.; Sistla, G.; Luley, C.J.; Crane, D.E. 2000. A modeling study of the impact of urban trees on ozone. Atmospheric Environment. 34: 1601–1613.

Nowak, D.J.; Crane, D.E. 2002. Carbon storage and sequestration by urban trees in the USA. Environmental Pollution. 116: 381–389.

Nowak, D.J.; Crane, D.E.; Stevens, J.C. 2006. Air pollution removal by urban trees and shrubs in the United States. Urban Forestry and Urban Greening. 4: 115–123.

Nowak, D.J.; Crane, D.E.; Stevens, J.C.; Ibarra, M. 2002. Brooklyn's urban forest. Gen. Tech. Rep. NE-290. Newtown Square, PA: U.S. Department of Agriculture, Forest Service, Northeastern Research Station. 107 p.

O'Brien, J.G.; Mielke, M.E.; Starkey, D.; Juzwik, J. 2000. How to identify, prevent, and control oak wilt. NA-PR-03-00. [Newtown Square, PA]: U.S. Department of Agriculture, Forest Service, Northeastern Area State and Private Forestry. 28 p.

Ottinger, R.L.; Wooley, D.R.; Robinson, N.A.; Hodas, D.R.; Babb, S.E. 1990. Environmental costs of electricity. New York: Oceana Publications. 769 p.

Parsons, R.; Tassinary, L.G.; Ulrich, R.S.; Hebl, M.R.; Grossman-Alexander, M. 1998. The view from the road: implications for stress recovery and immunization. Journal of Environmental Psychology. 18(2): 113–140.

Pearce, D. 2003. The social cost of carbon and its policy implications. Oxford Review of Economic Policy. 19(3): 362–384.

Peper, P.J.; McPherson, E.G. 2003. Evaluation of four methods for estimating leaf area of isolated trees. Urban Forestry and Urban Greening. 2(1): 19–29.

Peper, P.J.; McPherson, E.G.; Simpson, J.R.; Gardner, S.L.; Vargas, K.E.; Xiao, Q. [In press]. City of New York Municipal Forest Resource Assessment. Internal Tech. Rep. Davis, CA: U.S. Department of Agriculture, Forest Service, Pacific Southwest Research Station, Center for Urban Forest Research.

Pillsbury, N.H.; Reimer, J.L.; Thompson, R.P. 1998. Tree volume equations for fifteen urban species in California. Tech. Rep. 7. San Luis Obispo, CA: Urban Forest Ecosystems Institute, California Polytechnic State University. 56 p.

Platt, R.H.; Rowntree, R.A.; Muick, P.C., eds. 1994. The ecological city. Boston, MA: University of Massachusetts. 292 p.

Pokorny, J.D. 2003. Urban tree risk management: a community guide to program design and implementation. NA-TP-03-03. Newtown Square, PA: U.S. Department of Agriculture, Forest Service, Northeastern Area State and Private Forestry. [Pages unknown].

Ramsay, S. 2002. Personal communication. Executive Director, Trees Forever, 770 7th Ave., Marion, IA 52302.

Randrup, T.B.; McPherson, E.G.; Costello, L.R. 2001a. A review of tree root conflicts with sidewalks, curbs, and roads. Urban Ecosystems. 5: 209–225.

Randrup, T.B.; McPherson, E.G.; Costello, L.R. 2001b. Tree root intrusion in sewer systems: review of extent and costs. Journal of Infrastructure Systems. 7: 26–31.

Richards, N.A.; Mallette, J.R.; Simpson, R.J.; Macie, E.A. 1984. Residential greenspace and vegetation in a mature city: Syracuse, New York. Urban Ecology. 8: 99–125.

Rosenzweig, C.; Solecki, W.D.; Slosberg, R.B. 2006. Mitigating New York City's heat island with urban forestry, living roofs, and light surfaces. New York City, NY: Columbia University Center for Climate Systems Research and NASA/ Goddard Institute for Space Studies. 156 p. Final report for New York State Energy Research and Development Authority, Contract 6681.

Sand, M. 1991. Planting for energy conservation in the north. Minneapolis: Minnesota Department of Natural Resources. 19 p.

Sand, M. 1993. Energy saving landscapes: the Minnesota homeowner's guide. Minneapolis: Minnesota Department of Natural Resources. [Pages unknown].

Sand, M. 1994. Design and species selection to reduce urban heat islands and conserve energy. In: Proceedings from the sixth national urban forest conference: growing greener communities. Washington, DC: American Forests. 282 p.

Schroeder, H.W.; Cannon, W.N. 1983. The esthetic contribution of trees to residential streets in Ohio towns. Journal of Arboriculture. 9: 237–243.

Schroeder, T. 1982. The relationship of local park and recreation services to residential property values. Journal of Leisure Research. 14: 223–234.

Scott, K.I.; McPherson, E.G.; Simpson, J.R. 1998. Air pollutant uptake by Sacramento's urban forest. Journal of Arboriculture. 24(4): 224–234.

Scott, K.I.; Simpson, J.R.; McPherson, E.G. 1999. Effects of tree cover on parking lot microclimate and vehicle emissions. Journal of Arboriculture. 25(3): 129–142.

Simpson, J.R. 1998. Urban forest impacts on regional space conditioning energy use: Sacramento County case study. Journal of Arboriculture. 24(4): 201–214.

Smith, W.H. 1990. Air pollution and forests. New York: Springer-Verlag. 618 p.

Smith, W.H.; Dochinger, L.S. 1976. Capability of metropolitan trees to reduce atmospheric contaminants. In: Santamour, F.S.; Gerhold, H.D.; Little, S., eds. Better trees for metropolitan landscapes. Gen. Tech. Rep. NE-22. Upper Darby [Newtown Square], PA: U.S. Department of Agriculture, Forest Service, Northeastern Research Station: 49–60.

Sullivan, W.C.; Kuo, E.E. 1996. Do trees strengthen urban communities, reduce domestic violence? Arborist News. 5(2): 33–34.

Summit, J.; McPherson, E.G. 1998. Residential tree planting and care: a study of attitudes and behavior in Sacramento, California. Journal of Arboriculture. 24(2): 89–97.

Sydnor, T.D.; Gamstetter, D.; Nichols, J.; Bishop, B.; Favorite, J.; Blazer, C.; Turpin, L. 2000. Trees are not the root of sidewalk problems. Journal of Arboriculture. 26: 20–29.

Taha, H. 1996. Modeling impacts of increased urban vegetation on ozone air quality in the South Coast air basin. Atmospheric Environment. 30: 3423–3430.

Thompson, R.P.; Ahern, J.J. 2000. The state of urban and community forestry in California. San Luis Obispo, CA: Urban Forest Ecosystems Institute, California Polytechnic State University.

TreeLink. 2006. Log on, branch out. http://www.treelink.org/. (27 January 2007).

Tretheway, R.; Manthe, A. 1999. Skin cancer prevention: another good reason to plant trees. In: McPherson, E.G.; Mathis, S., eds. Proceedings of the Best of the West summit. Davis, CA: University of California: 72–75.

Tschantz, B.A.; Sacamano, P.L. 1994. Municipal tree management in the United States. Kent, OH: Davey Resource Group. 71 p.

Tyrvainen, L. 1999. Monetary valuation of urban forest amenities in Finland. Res. Pap. 739. Vantaa, Finland: Finnish Forest Research Institute. 129 p.

Ulrich, R.S. 1985. Human responses to vegetation and landscapes. Landscape and Urban Planning. 13: 29–44.

Urban, J. 1992. Bringing order to the technical dysfunction within the urban forest. Journal of Arboriculture. 18(2): 85–90.

U.S. Census Bureau. 2006. State and county quick facts. http://quickfacts.census. gov/qfd/states/08/08001.html. (July 2006).

U.S. Department of Agriculture, Natural Resource Conservation Service, Agroforestry Center [NRCS Agroforesty Center]. 2005. Working trees for treating waste. Western Arborist. 31: 50–52.

U.S. Environmental Protection Agency. 1998. Ap-42 compilation of air pollutant emission factors. 5th ed. Research Triangle Park, NC. [Pages unknown.]. Volume I.

U.S. Environmental Protection Agency. 2003. E-GRID (E-GRID2002 Edition). http://www.epa.gov/cleanenergy/egrid/index.htm. (2 June 2004).

U.S. Environmental Protection Agency. 2005. Green book: nonattainment areas for criteria pollutants. http://www.epa.gov/oar/oaqps/greenbk/index. html. (2 May 2005).

Wang, M.Q.; Santini, D.J. 1995. Monetary values of air pollutant emissions in various U.S. regions. Transportation Research Record. 1475: 33–41.

Watson, G.W.; Himelick, E.B. 1997. Principles and practice of planting trees and shrubs. Savoy, IL: International Society of Arboriculture. 199 p.

Wolf, K.L. 2005. Business district streetscapes, trees, and consumer response. Journal of Forestry. 103: 396–400.

Xiao, Q.; McPherson, E.G. 2002. Rainfall interception by Santa Monica's municipal urban forest. Urban Ecosystems. 6: 291–302.

Xiao, Q.; McPherson, E.G.; Simpson, J.R.; Ustin, S.L. 1998. Rainfall interception by Sacramento's urban forest. Journal of Arboriculture. 24(4): 235–244.

Xiao, Q.; McPherson, E.G.; Simpson, J.R.; Ustin, S.L. 2000. Winter rainfall interception by two mature open grown trees in Davis, California. Hydrological Processes. 14(4): 763–784.

Appendix 1: Additional Resources

Additional information regarding urban and community forestry program design and implementation can be found in the following sources:

Bratkovich, S.M. 2001. Utilizing municipal trees: ideas from across the country. NA-TP-06-01.

Miller, R.W. 1997. Urban forestry: planning and managing urban greenspaces. 2nd ed.

Morgan, N.R. [N.d.]. An introductory guide to community and urban forestry in Washington, Oregon, and California.

Morgan, N.R. 1993. A technical guide to urban and community forestry.

Pokorny, J.D., coord., author. 2003. Urban tree risk management: a community guide to program design and implementation. NA-TP-03-03.

For additional information on tree selection, planting, establishment, and care, see the following references:

Alliance for Community Trees: http://actrees.org.

Bedker, P.J.; O'Brien, J.G.; Mielke, M.E. 1995. How to prune trees. NA-FR-01-95.

Costello, L.R. 2000. Training Young Trees for Structure and Form. Videotape Number: V99-A.

Hargrave, R.; Johnson, G.R.; Zins, M.E. 2002. Planting trees and shrubs for long-term health. MI-07681-S.

Harris, R.W.; Clark, J.R.; Matheny, N.P. 2003. Arboriculture. 4th ed.

Hauer, R.J.; Hruska, M.C.; Dawson, J.O. 1994. Trees and ice storms: the development of ice storm-resistant urban tree populations. Spec. Publ. 94-1.

Haugen, L.M. 1998. How to identify and manage Dutch elm disease. NA-PR-07-98.

Hightshoe, G.L. 1988. Native trees, shrubs, and vines for urban and rural America.

Gilman, E.F. 1997. Trees for urban and suburban landscapes.

Gilman, E.F. 2002. An illustrated guide to pruning. 2nd ed.

International Society of Arboriculture: http://www.isa-arbor.com, including their Tree City USA Bulletin series.

National Arbor Day Foundation: http://www.arborday.org.

O'Brien, J.G.; Mielke, M.E.; Starkey, D.; Juzwik, J. 2000. How to identify, prevent, and control oak wilt. NA-PR-03-00.

TreeLink: http://www.treelink.org Trees for urban and suburban landscapes (Gilman 1997).

Urban Horticulture Institute: http://www.hort.cornell.edu/UHI/outreach/ recurbtree/index.html. Recommended urban trees: site assessment and tree selection for stress tolerance.

Watson, G.W.; Himelick, E.B. 1997. Principles and practice of planting trees and shrubs.

These suggested references are only a starting point. Your local cooperative extension agent or state forestry agency can provide you with up-to-date and local information.

Appendix 2: Benefit-Cost Information Tables

Information in this appendix can be used to estimate benefits and costs associated with proposed tree plantings. The tables contain data for representative small (Kwanzan cherry), medium (red maple), and large (Japanese zelkova) deciduous trees and a representative conifer (eastern white pine) (see "Common and Scientific Names" section). Data are presented as annual values for each 5-year interval after planting (tables 6–18). Annual values incorporate effects of tree loss. Based on the results of our survey, we assume that 34 percent of the trees planted die by the end of the 40-year period.

For the benefits tables (tables 6, 9, 12, 15), there are two columns for each 5-year interval. In the first column, values describe **resource units** (RUs): for example, the amount of air conditioning energy saved in kWh per year per tree, air pollutant uptake in pounds per year per tree, and rainfall intercepted in gallons per year per tree. Energy and carbon dioxide (CO_2) benefits for residential yard trees are broken out by tree location to show how shading effects differ among trees opposite west-, south-, and east-facing building walls. The second column for each 5-year interval contains dollar values obtained by multiplying RUs by local prices (e.g., kWh saved [RU] × \$/kWh).

In the costs tables (tables 7, 10, 13, 16), costs are broken down into categories for yard and public trees. Costs for yard trees do not differ by planting location (i.e., east, west, south walls). Although tree and planting costs occur at year 1, we divided this value by 5 years to derive an average annual cost for the first 5-year period. All other costs are the estimated values for each year and not values averaged over 5 years.

Total net benefits are calculated by subtracting total costs from total benefits and are presented in tables 8, 11, 14, and 17. Data are presented for a yard tree opposite west-, south-, and east-facing walls, as well as for the public tree.

The last column in each table presents 40-year-average annual values. These numbers were calculated by dividing the total costs and benefits by 40 years.

Table 6—Annual benefits at 5-year intervals and 40-year average for a representative small tree (Kwanzan cherry)

Benefits/tree	Year 5		Year 10		Year 15		Year 20		Year 25		Year 30		Year 35		Year 40		40-year average	
	RU	Value	RU	Value	RU	Value	RU	Value	RU	Value	RU	Value	RU	Value	RU	Value	RU	Value
		Dollars		Dollars		Dollars		Dollars		Dollars		Dollars		Dollars		Dollars		Dollars
Cooling (kWh)																		
Yard: west	4	0.57	11	1.61	19	2.66	27	3.72	34	4.70	40	5.55	45	6.31	50	6.99	29	4.01
Yard: south	3	0.47	8	1.05	12	1.65	16	2.26	20	2.81	24	3.35	28	3.85	31	4.31	18	2.47
Yard: east	4	0.55	10	1.43	17	2.35	24	3.29	30	4.17	36	4.99	41	5.75	46	6.43	26	3.62
Public	3	0.47	7	1.03	11	1.61	16	2.18	19	2.70	23	3.16	25	3.57	28	3.94	17	2.33
Heating (kBtu)																		
Yard: west	188	2.78	420	6.21	630	9.32	797	11.79	950	14.06	1,057	15.65	1,141	16.88	1,214	17.97	799	11.83
Yard: south	184	2.72	394	5.83	577	8.53	706	10.45	825	12.21	900	13.32	953	14.11	1,000	14.80	692	10.25
Yard: east	184	2.73	408	6.04	610	9.03	769	11.38	914	13.53	1,015	15.03	1,094	16.20	1,163	17.22	770	11.39
Public	190	2.82	429	6.35	647	9.58	823	12.18	984	14.57	1,098	16.26	1,189	17.59	1,268	18.77	829	12.26
Net energy (kBtu)																		
Yard: west	229	3.35	535	7.82	820	11.98	1,062	15.51	1,285	18.76	1,453	21.20	1,591	23.19	1,713	24.96	1,086	15.85
Yard: south	218	3.20	469	6.88	694	10.19	867	12.71	1,026	15.02	1,139	16.67	1,229	17.97	1,307	19.10	869	12.72
Yard: east	224	3.28	510	7.47	778	11.38	1,004	14.67	1,212	17.70	1,372	20.02	1,505	21.94	1,622	23.65	1,028	15.02
Public	224	3.29	503	7.39	762	11.19	978	14.36	1,177	17.27	1,324	19.42	1,443	21.16	1,549	22.70	995	14.60
Net carbon dioxide (lb)																		
Yard: west	29	0.10	70	0.23	110	0.37	145	0.48	178	0.60	206	0.69	230	0.77	252	0.84	153	0.51
Yard: south	28	0.09	63	0.21	96	0.32	124	0.41	150	0.50	171	0.57	190	0.63	207	0.69	129	0.43
Yard: east	29	0.10	68	0.23	105	0.35	139	0.46	170	0.57	197	0.66	220	0.74	242	0.81	146	0.49
Public	29	0.10	67	0.22	104	0.35	137	0.46	168	0.56	193	0.64	215	0.72	236	0.79	144	0.48
Air pollution (lb)[a]																		
Ozone uptake	0.023	0.11	0.059	0.27	0.094	0.43	0.126	0.58	0.159	0.73	0.188	0.86	0.215	0.99	0.242	1.11	0.14	0.63
Nitrogen dioxide uptake+avoided	0.036	0.16	0.084	0.38	0.129	0.59	0.169	0.78	0.207	0.95	0.238	1.09	0.265	1.22	0.290	1.33	0.18	0.81
Sulfur dioxide uptake+avoided	0.026	0.09	0.064	0.22	0.103	0.36	0.142	0.50	0.179	0.62	0.212	0.74	0.242	0.84	0.270	0.94	0.15	0.54
Small particulate matter uptake+avoided	0.012	0.10	0.048	0.40	0.094	0.78	0.145	1.20	0.188	1.56	0.191	1.59	0.194	1.61	0.196	1.63	0.13	1.11
Volatile organic compounds avoided	0.002	0.01	0.006	0.01	0.009	0.02	0.012	0.03	0.015	0.04	0.018	0.04	0.020	0.05	0.022	0.05	0.01	0.03
Biogenic volatile organic compounds released	-0.001	0.00	-0.001	0.00	-0.001	0.00	-0.002	0.00	-0.003	-0.01	-0.003	-0.01	-0.003	-0.01	-0.003	-0.01	0.00	0.00
Total air pollution avoided + uptake	0.099	0.47	0.260	1.29	0.428	2.18	0.593	3.08	0.745	3.89	0.843	4.31	0.932	4.69	1.016	5.05	0.61	3.12
Hydrology (gal)																		
Rainfall interception	60	0.48	142	1.14	226	1.81	312	2.49	397	3.18	486	3.89	575	4.60	664	5.31	358	2.86
Aesthetics and other																		
Yard		5.96		6.13		6.62		7.05		7.44		7.78		8.07		8.31		7.17
Public		6.67		6.87		7.41		7.90		8.33		8.71		9.03		9.31		8.03
Total benefits																		
Yard: west		10.36		16.62		22.95		28.62		33.87		37.86		41.32		44.48		29.51
Yard: south		10.20		15.65		21.11		25.74		30.04		33.22		35.96		38.48		26.30
Yard: east		10.28		16.26		22.33		27.76		32.78		36.66		40.04		43.13		28.66
Public		11.00		16.91		22.93		28.28		32.23		36.97		40.21		43.16		29.09

Note: Annual values incorporate effects of tree loss. We assume that 14 percent of trees planted die during the first 5 years and 19.95 percent during the remaining 35 years for a total mortality of 33.95 percent. RU = resource unit.

Table 7—Annual costs at 5-year intervals and 40-year average for a representative small tree (Kwanzan cherry)

Costs	Year 5	Year 10	Year 15	Year 20	Year 25	Year 30	Year 35	Year 40	40-year average
					Dollars				
Tree and planting									
Yard	120.00[a]								15.00
Public	80.00[a]								10.00
Pruning									
Yard	1.29	1.06	1.02	0.98	0.95	0.91	11.90	11.40	3.76
Public	2.58	2.91	2.81	2.71	2.61	2.51	4.82	4.62	3.26
Remove and dispose									
Yard	2.10	1.17	1.75	2.34	2.92	3.50	4.09	4.67	2.58
Public	2.38	0.48	0.73	0.97	1.21	1.45	1.69	1.93	1.28
Pest and disease									
Yard	0	0	0	0	0	0	0	0	0
Public	0.03	0.05	0.08	0.10	0.12	0.14	0.15	0.17	0.09
Infrastructure repair									
Yard	0.04	0.08	0.11	0.15	0.18	0.20	0.23	0.25	0.14
Public	0.32	0.62	0.90	1.16	1.40	1.62	1.81	1.98	1.13
Cleanup									
Yard	0.01	0.02	0.03	0.03	0.04	0.05	0.05	0.06	0.03
Public	0.07	0.14	0.20	0.26	0.32	0.36	0.41	0.45	0.26
Liability and legal									
Yard	0	0	0	0	0	0	0	0	0
Public	0	0	0	0	0	0	0	0	0
Admin./inspect/other									
Yard	0.40	0.77	1.11	1.43	1.72	1.99	2.23	2.44	1.51
Public	1.13	2.19	3.17	4.07	4.90	5.66	6.34	6.94	3.96
Total costs									
Yard	123.84	3.09	4.03	4.93	5.81	6.65	18.49	18.82	21.52
Public	86.52	6.40	7.89	9.27	10.56	11.73	15.22	16.09	19.99

Note: Annual values incorporate effects of tree loss. We assume that 14 percent of trees planted die during the first 5 years and 19.95 percent during the remaining 35 years for a total mortality of 33.95 percent.

[a]Although tree and planting costs occur in year 1, this value was divided by 5 years to derive an average annual cost for the first 5-year period.

Table 8—Annual net benefits at 5-year intervals and 40-year average for a representative small tree (Kwanzan cherry)

Total net benefits	Year 5	Year 10	Year 15	Year 20	Year 25	Year 30	Year 35	Year 40	40-year average
					Dollars				
Yard: west	-113	14	19	24	28	31	23	26	8
Yard: south	-114	13	17	21	24	27	17	20	5
Yard: east	-114	13	18	23	27	30	22	24	7
Public	-76	11	15	19	23	25	25	27	9

Note: Annual values incorporate effects of tree loss. We assume that 14 percent of trees planted die during the first 5 years, 19.95 percent during the remaining 35 years, for a total mortality of 33.95 percent.

See table 6 for annual benefits and table 7 for annual costs.

Table 9—Annual benefits at 5-year intervals and 40-year average for a representative medium tree (red maple)

Benefits/tree	Year 5		Year 10		Year 15		Year 20		Year 25		Year 30		Year 35		Year 40		40-year average	
	RU	Value	RU	Value	RU	Value	RU	Value	RU	Value	RU	Value	RU	Value	RU	Value	RU	Value
		Dollars		Dollars		Dollars		Dollars		Dollars		Dollars		Dollars		Dollars		Dollars
Cooling (kWh)																		
Yard: west	8	1.07	22	3.09	47	6.59	71	9.95	94	13.16	115	16.10	131	18.32	143	19.97	79	11.03
Yard: south	4	0.62	13	1.80	26	3.64	39	5.52	55	7.74	70	9.77	82	11.44	92	12.89	48	6.68
Yard: east	6	0.87	19	2.68	43	5.96	65	9.10	86	12.09	106	14.83	120	16.84	130	18.22	72	10.07
Public	4	0.61	12	1.70	23	3.16	33	4.62	45	6.25	55	7.75	64	9.04	73	10.25	39	5.42
Heating (kBtu)																		
Yard: west	239	3.54	619	9.16	1,054	15.60	1,450	21.47	1,764	26.11	2,050	30.35	2,260	33.45	2,406	35.62	1,480	21.91
Yard: south	221	3.27	544	8.05	820	12.13	1,076	15.93	1,301	19.26	1,506	22.29	1,661	24.59	1,779	26.34	1,114	16.48
Yard: east	229	3.39	592	8.77	1,006	14.89	1,385	20.50	1,695	25.09	1,979	29.29	2,183	32.32	2,323	34.38	1,424	21.08
Public	246	3.64	642	9.50	1,109	16.42	1,534	22.71	1,869	27.66	2,174	32.18	2,400	35.52	2,562	37.92	1,567	23.19
Net energy (kBtu)																		
Yard: west	315	4.60	839	12.24	1,525	22.20	2,161	31.42	2,703	39.27	3,199	46.44	3,567	51.76	3,832	55.58	2,268	32.94
Yard: south	266	3.90	673	9.85	1,079	15.77	1,471	21.46	1,853	27.00	2,204	32.06	2,478	36.03	2,700	39.23	1,590	23.16
Yard: east	291	4.26	784	11.45	1,432	20.85	2,034	29.60	2,558	37.18	3,037	44.12	3,385	49.15	3,623	52.60	2,143	31.15
Public	290	4.25	763	11.20	1,335	19.58	1,864	27.33	2,315	33.91	2,727	39.93	3,045	44.56	3,294	48.18	1,954	28.62
Net carbon dioxide (lb)																		
Yard: west	43	0.15	112	0.37	195	0.65	271	0.91	335	1.12	393	1.31	434	1.45	462	1.54	281	0.94
Yard: south	38	0.13	94	0.31	145	0.49	195	0.65	240	0.80	282	0.94	313	1.05	336	1.12	205	0.69
Yard: east	41	0.14	106	0.35	184	0.62	257	0.86	319	1.06	375	1.25	415	1.38	439	1.47	267	0.89
Public	41	0.14	104	0.35	176	0.59	242	0.81	296	0.99	346	1.16	383	1.28	409	1.36	250	0.83
Air pollution (lb)[a]																		
Ozone uptake	0.029	0.14	0.087	0.40	0.164	0.75	0.243	1.12	0.326	1.49	0.408	1.87	0.486	2.23	0.565	2.60	0.29	1.32
Nitrogen dioxide uptake+avoided	0.046	0.21	0.127	0.59	0.233	1.07	0.335	1.54	0.432	1.98	0.524	2.40	0.600	2.75	0.666	3.06	0.37	1.70
Sulfur dioxide uptake + avoided	0.039	0.13	0.113	0.39	0.233	0.81	0.350	1.22	0.470	1.64	0.582	2.03	0.671	2.34	0.744	2.59	0.40	1.39
Small particulate matter uptake + avoided	0.008	0.07	0.049	0.40	0.135	1.12	0.261	2.17	0.389	3.23	0.516	4.29	0.639	5.31	0.645	5.36	0.33	2.74
Volatile organic compounds avoided	0.004	0.01	0.010	0.02	0.019	0.04	0.028	0.07	0.037	0.09	0.045	0.10	0.051	0.12	0.056	0.13	0.03	0.07
Biogenic volatile organic compounds released	-0.002	0.00	-0.033	-0.08	-0.069	-0.16	-0.118	-0.27	-0.170	-0.39	-0.225	-0.52	-0.284	-0.66	-0.284	-0.66	-0.15	-0.34
Total air pollution avoided + net uptake	0.124	0.55	0.352	1.73	0.715	3.64	1.099	5.83	1.484	8.04	1.849	10.17	2.163	12.09	2.393	13.07	1.27	6.89
Hydrology (gal)																		
Rainfall interception	147	1.18	434	3.47	721	5.77	1,014	8.11	1,305	10.44	1,596	12.77	1,873	14.98	2,156	17.25	1,156	9.25
Aesthetics and other																		
Yard		35.75		32.41		31.15		29.84		28.48		27.08		25.66		24.21		29.32
Public		40.03		36.30		34.88		33.41		31.89		30.33		28.73		27.12		32.84
Total benefits																		
Yard: west		42.23		50.22		63.41		76.10		87.34		97.78		105.94		111.66		79.34
Yard: south		41.51		47.77		56.82		65.89		74.76		83.03		89.81		94.89		69.31
Yard: east		41.88		49.41		62.03		74.24		85.20		95.39		103.27		108.60		77.50
Public		46.16		53.04		64.46		75.49		85.27		94.35		101.64		106.98		78.42

Note: Annual values incorporate effects of tree loss. We assume that 14 percent of trees planted die during the first 5 years and 19.95 percent during the remaining 35 years for a total mortality of 33.95 percent. RU = resource unit.

Table 10—Annual costs at 5-year intervals and 40-year average for a representative medium tree (red maple)

Costs	Year 5	Year 10	Year 15	Year 20	Year 25	Year 30	Year 35	Year 40	40-year average
					Dollars				
Tree and planting									
Yard	120.00[a]								15.00
Public	80.00[a]								10.00
Pruning									
Yard	1.29	1.06	13.87	13.38	12.89	12.39	26.44	25.34	12.52
Public	2.58	2.91	5.62	5.42	5.22	5.02	19.28	18.48	7.69
Remove and dispose									
Yard	2.10	1.68	2.48	3.25	4.00	4.73	5.43	6.11	3.45
Public	2.38	0.70	1.03	1.35	1.66	1.96	2.25	2.53	1.62
Pest and disease									
Yard	0	0	0	0	0	0	0	0	0
Public	0.04	0.08	0.11	0.14	0.16	0.18	0.20	0.22	0.13
Infrastructure repair									
Yard	0.06	0.11	0.16	0.20	0.24	0.27	0.25	0.32	0.19
Public	0.48	0.90	1.28	1.62	1.92	2.18	2.41	2.59	1.55
Cleanup									
Yard	0.01	0.03	0.04	0.05	0.05	0.06	0.06	0.07	0.04
Public	0.11	0.20	0.29	0.37	0.43	0.49	0.54	0.58	0.35
Liability and legal									
Yard	0	0	0	0	0	0	0	0	0
Public	0	0	0	0	0	0	0	0	0
Admin/inspect/other									
Yard	0.59	1.11	1.58	1.99	2.36	2.69	2.50	3.19	1.90
Public	1.67	3.15	4.48	5.67	6.72	7.64	8.42	9.08	5.42
Total costs									
Yard	124.05	3.98	18.13	18.88	19.55	20.14	34.68	35.04	33.11
Public	87.25	7.93	12.81	14.56	16.12	17.47	33.10	33.49	26.76

Note: Annual values incorporate effects of tree loss. We assume that 14 percent of trees planted die during the first 5 years and 19.95 percent during the remaining 35 years for a total mortality of 33.95 percent.

[a]Although tree and planting costs occur in year 1, this value was divided by 5 years to derive an average annual cost for the first 5-year period.

Table 11—Annual net benefits at 5-year intervals and 40-year average for a representative medium tree (red maple)

Total net benefits	Year 5	Year 10	Year 15	Year 20	Year 25	Year 30	Year 35	Year 40	40-year average
					Dollars				
Yard: west	-82	46	45	57	68	78	71	77	46
Yard: south	-83	44	39	47	55	63	55	60	36
Yard: east	-82	45	44	55	66	75	69	74	44
Public	-41	45	52	61	69	77	69	73	52

Note: Annual values incorporate effects of tree loss. We assume that 14 percent of trees planted die during the first 5 years and 19 95 percent during the remaining 35 years for a total mortality of 33.95 percent.

See table 9 for annual benefits and table 10 for annual costs.

Table 12—Annual benefits at 5-year intervals and 40-year average for a representative large tree (Japanese zelkova)

Benefits/tree	Year 5 RU	Year 5 Value	Year 10 RU	Year 10 Value	Year 15 RU	Year 15 Value	Year 20 RU	Year 20 Value	Year 25 RU	Year 25 Value	Year 30 RU	Year 30 Value	Year 35 RU	Year 35 Value	Year 40 RU	Year 40 Value	40-year average RU	40-year average Value
		Dollars		Dollars		Dollars		Dollars		Dollars		Dollars		Dollars		Dollars		Dollars
Cooling (kWh)																		
Yard: west	54	7.55	106	14.81	150	21.01	176	24.73	196	27.44	208	29.08	216	30.19	221	30.96	166	23.22
Yard: south	30	4.23	62	8.68	92	12.85	115	16.16	134	18.77	150	21.03	162	22.70	172	24.07	115	16.06
Yard: east	49	6.88	95	13.37	134	18.81	157	22.04	174	24.44	186	26.07	194	27.18	201	28.16	149	20.87
Public	26	3.69	50	6.99	72	10.03	89	12.47	103	14.38	114	15.97	122	17.13	130	18.27	88	12.37
Heating (kBtu)																		
Yard: west	1,182	17.50	1,900	28.12	2,449	36.24	2,768	40.97	3,001	44.42	3,155	46.70	3,257	48.21	3,310	48.98	2,628	38.89
Yard: south	810	11.99	1,189	17.60	1,487	22.01	1,705	25.23	1,874	27.74	2,028	30.02	2,138	31.64	2,225	32.93	1,682	24.89
Yard: east	1,085	16.06	1,759	26.04	2,286	33.83	2,603	38.52	2,838	42.00	3,006	44.50	3,120	46.19	3,186	47.15	2,485	36.79
Public	1,289	19.08	2,100	31.09	2,722	40.29	3,076	45.53	3,335	49.36	3,503	51.85	3,613	53.47	3,662	54.21	2,913	43.11
Net energy (kBtu)																		
Yard: west	1,721	25.05	2,957	42.93	3,948	57.25	4,533	65.70	4,960	71.86	5,231	75.79	5,412	78.40	5,519	79.95	4,285	62.12
Yard: south	1,112	16.22	1,809	26.28	2,404	34.85	2,858	41.39	3,214	46.51	3,530	51.05	3,758	54.35	3,943	57.00	2,828	40.96
Yard: east	1,577	22.95	2,713	39.41	3,628	52.64	4,176	60.57	4,583	66.45	4,867	70.56	5,061	73.37	5,196	75.31	3,975	57.66
Public	1,552	22.76	2,599	38.07	3,437	50.31	3,967	58.01	4,361	63.74	4,643	67.81	4,836	70.60	4,967	72.48	3,795	55.47
Net carbon dioxide (lb)																		
Yard: west	204	0.68	357	1.19	483	1.61	563	1.88	621	2.08	657	2.19	682	2.28	686	2.29	532	1.78
Yard: south	136	0.45	229	0.76	310	1.04	374	1.25	425	1.42	465	1.55	495	1.65	508	1.70	368	1.23
Yard: east	188	0.63	330	1.10	448	1.50	523	1.75	580	1.94	617	2.06	644	2.15	651	2.17	498	1.66
Public	188	0.63	323	1.08	435	1.45	509	1.70	564	1.89	601	2.01	628	2.10	634	2.12	485	1.62
Air pollution (lb)[a]																		
Ozone uptake	0.068	0.31	0.199	0.91	0.337	1.55	0.489	2.24	0.624	2.86	0.761	3.49	0.881	4.04	0.999	4.59	0.54	2.50
Nitrogen dioxide uptake + avoided	0.210	0.96	0.397	1.82	0.565	2.59	0.699	3.21	0.808	3.71	0.905	4.15	0.982	4.51	1.051	4.83	0.70	3.22
Sulfur dioxide uptake + avoided	0.248	0.86	0.495	1.72	0.716	2.49	0.874	3.04	0.997	3.47	1.093	3.81	1.165	4.06	1.229	4.28	0.85	2.97
Small particulate matter uptake + avoided	0.032	0.26	0.097	0.80	0.212	1.76	0.369	3.06	0.525	4.36	0.677	5.62	0.824	6.84	0.828	6.88	0.45	3.70
Volatile organic compounds avoided	0.022	0.05	0.041	0.09	0.057	0.13	0.068	0.16	0.076	0.18	0.082	0.19	0.086	0.20	0.089	0.21	0.06	0.15
Biogenic volatile organic compounds released	0.000	0.00	0.000	0.00	0.000	0.00	0.000	0.00	0.000	0.00	0.000	0.00	0.000	0.00	0.000	0.00	0.00	0.00
Total air pollution avoided + net uptake	0.578	2.45	1.229	5.36	1.888	8.53	2.498	11.72	3.030	14.58	3.517	17.27	3.937	19.65	4.196	20.78	2.61	12.54
Hydrology (gal)																		
Rainfall interception	245	1.96	651	5.21	1,095	8.76	1,624	12.99	2,112	16.89	2,672	21.38	3,163	25.30	3,708	29.67	1,909	15.27
Aesthetics and other																		
Yard		38.87		46.39		53.60		58.46		61.26		62.26		61.71		59.85		55.30
Public		43.53		51.95		60.03		65.47		68.61		69.72		69.11		67.03		61.93
Total benefits																		
Yard: west		69.01		101.09		129.76		150.75		166.67		178.88		187.33		192.53		147.00
Yard: south		59.95		84.00		106.78		125.81		140.67		153.51		162.66		168.99		125.30
Yard: east		66.85		97.47		125.03		145.49		161.12		173.53		182.18		187.78		142.43
Public		71.33		101.68		129.09		149.89		165.71		178.19		186.76		192.07		146.84

Note: Annual values incorporate effects of tree loss. We assume that 14 percent of trees planted die during the first 5 years, 19.95 percent during the remaining 35 years, for a total mortality of 33.95 percent. RU = resource unit.

Table 13—Annual costs at 5-year intervals and 40-year average for a representative large tree (Japanese zelkova)

Costs	Year 5	Year 10	Year 15	Year 20	Year 25	Year 30	Year 35	Year 40	40-year average
					Dollars				
Tree and planting									
Yard	120.00[a]								15.00
Public	80.00[a]								10.00
Pruning									
Yard	1.29	14.37	13.87	13.38	28.64	27.54	26.44	25.34	18.01
Public	2.58	5.82	5.62	5.42	20.88	20.08	19.28	18.48	11.60
Remove and dispose									
Yard	5.80	2.31	3.38	4.40	5.35	6.25	7.09	7.87	4.61
Public	2.40	0.96	1.40	1.82	2.22	2.59	2.93	3.26	2.06
Pest and disease									
Yard	0	0	0	0	0	0	0	0	0
Public	0.05	0.10	0.15	0.18	0.22	0.24	0.26	0.28	0.17
Infrastructure repair									
Yard	0.08	0.15	0.22	0.27	0.32	0.36	0.39	0.42	0.26
Public	0.66	1.24	1.75	2.19	2.57	2.88	3.14	3.34	2.06
Clean-up									
Yard	0.02	0.03	0.05	0.06	0.07	0.08	0.09	0.09	0.06
Public	0.15	0.28	0.39	0.49	0.58	0.65	0.71	0.75	0.46
Liability and legal									
Yard	0	0	0	0	0	0	0	0	0
Public	0	0	0	0	0	0	0	0	0
Admin./inspect/other									
Yard	0.81	1.52	2.15	2.70	3.16	3.55	3.86	3.68	2.54
Public	2.29	4.33	6.12	7.67	8.99	10.10	10.99	11.70	7.21
Total costs									
Yard	128.00	18.39	19.68	20.81	37.54	37.78	37.88	37.41	40.47
Public	88.13	12.73	15.43	17.78	35.45	36.54	37.32	37.81	33.57

Note: Annual values incorporate effects of tree loss. We assume that 14 percent of trees planted die during the first 5 years and 19.95 percent during the remaining 35 years for a total mortality of 33.95 percent.

[a]Although tree and planting costs occur in year 1, this value was divided by 5 years to derive an average annual cost for the first 5-year period.

Table 14—Annual net benefits at 5-year intervals and 40-year average for a representative large tree (Japanese zelkova)

Total net benefits	Year 5	Year 10	Year 15	Year 20	Year 25	Year 30	Year 35	Year 40	40-year average
					Dollars				
Yard: west	-59	83	110	130	129	141	149	155	107
Yard: south	-68	66	87	105	103	116	125	132	85
Yard: east	-61	79	105	125	124	136	144	150	102
Public	-17	89	114	132	130	142	149	154	113

Note: Annual values incorporate effects of tree loss. We assume that 14 percent of trees planted die during the first 5 years and 19.95 percent during the remaining 35 years for a total mortality of 33 95 percent.

See table 12 for annual benefits and table 13 for annual costs.

Table 15—Annual benefits at 5-year intervals and 40-year average for a representative conifer (eastern white pine) planted as a windbreak tree in a location that will not shade buildings

Benefits/tree	Year 5		Year 10		Year 15		Year 20		Year 25		Year 30		Year 35		Year 40		40-year average	
	RU	Value	RU	Value	RU	Value	RU	Value	RU	Value	RU	Value	RU	Value	RU	Value	RU	Value
		Dollars		Dollars		Dollars		Dollars		Dollars		Dollars		Dollars		Dollars		Dollars
Cooling (kWh)	3	0.40	8	1.05	15	2.08	22	3.05	29	4.09	37	5 15	43	5.98	48	6.77	25	3.57
Heating (kBtu)	278	4.11	653	9.66	1,095	16.20	1,507	22.30	1,831	27 10	2,123	31.43	2,348	34.75	2,538	37.57	1,547	22.89
Net energy (kBtu)	306	4.51	728	10.71	1,243	18.29	1,724	25.35	2,123	31.20	2,491	36.57	2,774	40.72	3,022	44.34	1,801	26.46
Net carbon dioxide (lb)	37	0.12	89	0.30	152	0.51	211	0.70	258	0.86	301	1.01	334	1.12	364	1.21	218	0.73
Air pollution (lb)																		
Ozone uptake	0.024	0 11	0.073	0.34	0.152	0.70	0.232	1.07	0.316	1.45	0.404	1.85	0.482	2.21	0.561	2.58	0.28	1.29
Nitrogen dioxide uptake + avoided	0.045	0.21	0.115	0.53	0.210	0.97	0.303	1.39	0.389	1.78	0.474	2 17	0.544	2.50	0.611	2.81	0.34	1.54
Sulfur dioxide uptake + avoided	0.024	0.08	0.065	0.23	0.130	0.45	0.193	0.67	0.260	0.90	0.328	114	0.385	1.34	0.440	1.53	0.23	0.79
Small particulate matter uptake + avoided	0.007	0.06	0.056	0.46	0.175	1.45	0.366	3.04	0.572	4.75	0.577	4.80	0.582	4.83	0.586	4.87	0.37	3.03
Volatile organic compounds avoided	0.003	0.01	0.007	0.02	0.012	0.03	0.017	0.04	0.022	0.05	0.026	0.06	0.030	0.07	0.033	0.08	0.02	0.04
Biogenic volatile organic compounds released	-0.020	-0.05	-0.264	-0.61	-0.579	-1.34	-1.077	-2.49	-1.663	-3.85	-1.663	-3.85	-1.663	-3.85	-1.663	-3.85	-1.07	-2.49
Total air pollution avoided + uptake	0.082	0.42	0.051	0.95	0.101	2.26	0.034	3.72	-0.106	5.09	0.146	6 18	0.359	7.10	0.568	8.01	0.15	4.22
Hydrology (gal)																		
Rainfall interception	103	0.83	320	2.56	553	4.42	786	6.29	1,024	8 19	1,273	10 18	1,494	11.95	1,721	13.77	909	7.27
Aesthetics and other																		
Yard		1710		16.22		16 12		15.82		15.34		14.71		13.96		13.10		15.30
Public		1915		18.16		18.05		1771		1718		16.48		15.63		14.67		17.13
Total benefits																		
Yard		22.98		30.74		41.59		51.88		60.68		68.65		74.85		80.43		53.98
Public		25.03		32.69		43.52		53.77		62.52		70.42		76.53		82.00		55.81

Note: Annual values incorporate effects of tree loss. We assume that 14 percent of trees planted die during the first 5 years, 19.95 percent during the remaining 35 years, for a total mortality of 33.95 percent. RU=resource unit.

Table 16—Annual costs at 5-year intervals and 40-year average for a representative conifer (eastern white pine)

Costs	Year 5	Year 10	Year 15	Year 20	Year 25	Year 30	Year 35	Year 40	40-year average
					Dollars				
Tree and planting									
Yard	120.00[a]								15.00
Public	80.00[a]								10.00
Pruning									
Yard	1.29	1.06	13.87	13.38	12.89	27.54	26.44	25.34	14.31
Public	2.58	2.91	5.62	5.42	5.22	5.02	4.82	18.48	6.40
Remove and dispose									
Yard	5.80	1.53	2.24	2.91	3.55	4.15	4.72	5.25	3.07
Public	2.40	0.63	0.93	1.20	1.47	1.72	1.95	2.17	1.47
Pest and disease									
Yard	0	0	0	0	0	0	0	0	0
Public	0.05	0.07	0.10	0.12	0.14	0.16	0.18	0.19	0.11
Infrastructure repair									
Yard	0.08	0.10	0.14	0.18	0.21	0.24	0.26	0.28	0.17
Public	0.66	0.82	1.15	1.45	1.70	1.91	2.09	2.23	1.37
Cleanup									
Yard	0.02	0.02	0.03	0.04	0.05	0.05	0.06	0.06	0.04
Public	0.15	0.18	0.26	0.33	0.38	0.43	0.47	0.50	0.31
Liability and legal									
Yard	0	0	0	0	0	0	0	0	0
Public	0	0	0	0	0	0	0	0	0
Admin/inspect/other									
Yard	0	0	0	0	0	0	0	0	0
Public	2.29	0.98	2.62	3.29	3.86	4.35	4.75	5.06	3.10
Total costs									
Yard	128.00	2.71	16.29	16.51	16.69	31.98	31.48	34.62	32.59
Public	88.13	5.59	10.68	11.81	12.78	13.60	14.26	28.64	22.76

Note: Annual values incorporate effects of tree loss. We assume that 14 percent of trees planted die during the first 5 years and 19.95 percent during the remaining 35 years for a total mortality of 33.95 percent.

[a]Although tree and planting costs occur in year 1, this value was divided by 5 years to derive an average annual cost for the first 5-year period.

Table 17—Annual net benefits at 5-year intervals and 40-year average for a representative conifer (eastern white pine) planted as a windbreak tree in a location that will not shade buildings

Total net benefits	Year 5	Year 10	Year 15	Year 20	Year 25	Year 30	Year 35	Year 40	40-year average
					Dollars				
Yard	-105	28	25	35	44	37	43	46	21
Public	-63	27	33	42	50	57	62	53	33

Note: Annual values incorporate effects of tree loss. We assume that 14 percent of trees planted die during the first 5 years and 19.95 percent during the remaining 35 years for a total mortality of 33.95 percent.

See table 15 for annual benefits and table 16 for annual costs.

Table 18—Emission factors and implied values

	Emission factor		Implied value
	Electricity	Natural gas	
	lbs/MWh	*lbs/MBtu*	*$/lb*
Carbon dioxide	1,030.000	118.0000	0.00334
Nitrogen dioxide	1.745	0.1020	4.59
Sulfur dioxide	5.928	0.0006	3.48
Small particulate matter	0.462	0.0075	8.31
Volatile organic compounds	0.401	0.0054	2.31

Appendix 3: Procedures for Estimating Benefits and Costs

Approach

Overview

Because benefits from trees differ owing to regional differences in tree growth, climate, air pollutant concentrations, rainfall patterns, building characteristics, and other factors, we divided the United States into 20 climate zones. A reference city is designated for each climate zone, and intensive data are collected for modeling tree benefits. Criteria for selection as a reference city include:

- Updated inventory of trees by address.

- Detailed information on tree management costs.

- Long-tenured city foresters who can help age trees because they know when they were planted or when different neighborhoods were developed and street trees planted.

- Good contacts within other city departments to obtain data on sidewalk repair costs, trip/fall costs, and litter cleanup costs.

- Capability to provide the resources needed to conduct the study, including an aerial lift truck for 5 days to sample foliar biomass.

The Borough of Queens was selected as the reference city for the Northeast region because it best met these criteria. During 2005, data were collected on tree growth and size for predominant street tree species in Queens, and other geographic information was assembled to model tree benefits. A subset of these data is used in this guide, and the entire data set is incorporated into the i-Tree STRATUM database for the Northeast region (see www.itreetools.org).

In this study, annual benefits and costs over a 40-year planning horizon were estimated for newly planted trees in three residential yard locations (east, south, and west of the dwelling unit) and a public street-side or park location. Trees in these hypothetical locations are called "yard" and "public" trees, respectively. Prices were assigned to each cost (e.g. planting, pruning, removal, irrigation, infrastructure repair, liability) and benefit (e.g., heating/cooling, energy savings, air-pollution reduction, stormwater-runoff reduction) through direct estimation and implied valuation of benefits as environmental externalities. This approach made it possible to estimate the net benefits of plantings in "typical" locations with "typical" tree species.

To account for differences in the mature size and growth rates of different tree species, we report results for a small (Kwanzan cherry), medium (red maple), and large (Japanese zelkova) deciduous tree and for a conifer (eastern white pine) (see "Common and Scientific Names" section). The selection of these species was based on data availability, and not intended to endorse their use in large numbers. In fact, the Kwanzan cherry has a poor form for a street tree and in certain areas zelkova is overused. Relying on too few species can increase the likelihood of catastrophic loss owing to pests, diseases, or other threats. Results are reported for 5-year intervals for 40 years.

Mature tree height is frequently used to characterize small, medium, and large species because matching tree height to available overhead space is an important design consideration. However, in this analysis, leaf surface area (LSA) and crown diameter were also used to characterize **mature tree size**. These additional measurements are useful indicators for many functional benefits of trees that relate to leaf-atmosphere processes (e.g., interception, transpiration, photosynthesis). Tree growth rates, dimensions, and LSA estimates are based on tree growth modeling.

Growth Modeling

Growth models are based on data collected in the Borough of Queens, New York City. An inventory of Queens' street trees was provided by the City of New York Department of Parks and Recreation. The inventory was conducted in 1995 and updated to account for dead tree removals and new plantings. It included 255,742 trees representing 242 species.

Tree-growth models developed from Borough of Queens data were used as the basis for modeling tree growth for this report. Using Queens' tree inventory, a stratified random sample of 21 tree species was measured to establish relations among tree age, size, leaf area, and biomass.

For the growth models, information spanning the life cycle of predominant tree species was collected. The inventory was stratified into the following nine diameter-at-breast-height (d.b.h.) classes:

1. 0–2.9 in

2. 3–5.9 in

3. 6–11.9 in

4. 12–17.9 in

5. 18–23.9 in

6. 24–29.9 in

7. 30–35.9 in

8. 36–41.9 in

9. ≥ 42 in

Thirty to 60 trees of each species were randomly selected for surveying, along with an equal number of alternative trees. Tree measurements included d.b.h. (to nearest 0.1 cm by sonar measuring device), tree crown and bole height (to nearest 0.5 m by clinometer), crown diameter in two directions (parallel and perpendicular to nearest street to nearest 0.5 m by sonar measuring device), tree condition and location. Replacement trees were sampled when trees from the original sample population could not be located. A total of 910 trees were measured. Field work was conducted in August 2005.

Tree coring was used in Queens to estimate planting dates instead of using historical research conducted in other reference cities. Unlike other cities, where even-aged stands exist along streets planted at the time of development, street trees in Queens were of all ages because several generations had come and gone. Dr. Brendan Buckley of Lamont-Doherty Earth Observatory's Tree Ring Laboratory, supervised the coring of 150 randomly sampled trees to establish mean tree age. These trees represented a subsample of the original 910 sample trees. One to two trees in size classes 2 through 9 were cored for each species. Coring was conducted from October 2005 through April 2006. Cores were analyzed in the lab and tree age established. Central Forestry and Horticulture provided tree ages for an additional 104 sample trees in d.b.h. classes 8 and 9, based on building records, and 34 trees in d.b.h. classes 1 and 2 based on planting records. These data were pooled with ring-count data to develop regressions based on the mean age for each d.b.h. size class.

Crown volume and leaf area were estimated from computer processing of tree-crown images obtained by using a digital camera. The method has shown greater accuracy than other techniques (±20 percent of actual leaf area) in estimating crown volume and leaf area of open-grown trees (Peper and McPherson 2003).

Linear regression was used to fit predictive models with d.b.h. as a function of age for each of the 21 sampled species. Predictions of LSA, crown diameter, and height metrics were modeled as a function of d.b.h. by using best-fit models. After inspecting the growth curves for each species, we selected the typical small, medium, and large tree species for this report.

The conifer is included as a windbreak tree located more than 50 ft from the residence, so it does not shade the building. Tree dimensions are derived from growth curves developed from street trees in the Borough of Queens, New York City (Peper et al., in press) (fig. 17).

Reporting Results

Results are reported in terms of annual values per tree planted. However, to make these calculations realistic, mortality rates are included. Based on our survey of regional municipal foresters and commercial arborists, this analysis assumed that

34 percent of the hypothetical planted trees died over the 40-year period. Annual mortality rates were 2.8 percent for the first 5 years, and 0.57 percent per year after that. This accounting approach "grows" trees in different locations and uses computer simulation to directly calculate the annual flow of benefits and costs as trees mature and die (McPherson 1992).

Benefits and costs are directly connected with tree-size variables such as trunk d.b.h., tree canopy cover, and LSA. For instance, pruning and removal costs usually increase with tree size, expressed as d.b.h. For some parameters, such as sidewalk repair, costs are negligible for young trees but increase relatively rapidly as tree roots grow large enough to heave pavement. For other parameters, such as air-pollutant uptake and rainfall interception, benefits are related to tree canopy cover and leaf area.

Most benefits occur on an annual basis, but some costs are periodic. For instance, street trees may be pruned on regular cycles but are removed in a less regular fashion (e.g., when they pose a hazard or soon after they die). In this analysis, most costs and benefits are reported for the year in which they occur. However, periodic costs such as pruning, pest and disease control, and infrastructure repair are presented on an average annual basis. Although spreading one-time costs over each year of a maintenance cycle does not alter the 40-year nominal expenditure, it can lead to inaccuracies if future costs are discounted to the present.

Benefit and Cost Valuation
Source of cost estimates

Frequency and costs of tree management were estimated based on surveys with municipal foresters from Fairfield and Mansfield, Connecticut, as well as the Borough of Queens, New York City. In addition, commercial arborists in the New York metropolitan region provided information on tree management costs on residential properties.

Pricing benefits

Electricity and natural-gas prices for utilities serving Queens were used to quantify energy savings for the region. Costs of preventing or repairing damage from pollution, flooding, or other environmental risks were used to estimate what society is willing to pay for clean air and water (Wang and Santini 1995). For example, the value of stormwater runoff reduction owing to rainfall interception by trees is estimated by using marginal control costs. If a community or developer is willing to pay an average of $0.01 per gallon of treated and controlled runoff to meet minimum standards, then the stormwater runoff mitigation value of a tree that intercepts 1,000 gallon of rainfall, eliminating the need for control, should be $10.

Calculating Benefits

Calculating Energy Benefits—

The prototypical building used as a basis for the simulations was typical of post-1980 construction practices, and represents approximately one-third of the total single-family residential housing stock in the Northeast region. The house was a one-story, wood-frame, building with a basement and total conditioned floor area of 2,090 ft², window area (double-glazed) of 262 ft2, and wall and ceiling insulation of R13 and R27, respectively. The central cooling system had a **seasonal energy efficiency ratio (SEER)** of 10, and the natural-gas furnace had an **annual fuel utilization efficiency (AFUE)** of 78 percent. Building footprints were square, reflecting average impacts for a large number of buildings (McPherson and Simpson 1999). Buildings were simulated with 1.5-ft overhangs. Blinds had a visual density of 37 percent and were assumed to be closed when the air conditioner was operating. Summer thermostat settings were 78 °F; winter settings were 68 °F during the day and 60 °F at night. Because the prototype building was larger, but more energy efficient, than most other construction types, our projected energy savings can be considered similar to those for older, less thermally efficient, but smaller buildings. The energy simulations relied on typical meteorological data from New York City (Marion and Urban 1995).

Calculating energy savings—

The dollar value of energy savings was based on regional average residential electricity and natural-gas prices of $0.14/kWh and $1.48/therm, respectively. Electricity and natural-gas prices were for 2006 for New York City (Con Edison 2006a and 2006b, respectively). Homes were assumed to have central air conditioning and natural-gas heating.

Calculating shade effects—

Residential yard trees were within 60 ft of homes so as to directly shade walls and windows. Shade effects of these trees on building energy use were simulated for small, medium, and large deciduous trees and a conifer at three tree-to-building distances, following methods outlined by McPherson and Simpson (1999). The small tree (Kwanzan cherry) had a visual density of 75 percent during summer and 20 percent during winter. The medium tree (red maple) had a density of 73 percent during summer and 17 percent during winter. The large tree (Japanese zelkova) had a visual density of 74 percent during summer and 15 percent during winter, and the conifer (eastern white pine) had a density of 28 percent year round. Crown densities for calculating shade were based on published values where available (Hammond et al. 1980, McPherson 1984).

Foliation periods for deciduous trees were obtained from the literature (Hammond et al. 1980, McPherson 1984) and adjusted for New York City's climate based on consultation with the Central Forestry and Horticulture project coordinator and borough forestry directors (Lu 2006). Large trees were leafless November 1 through May 1, medium and small trees November 15 through May 4, and conifers were evergreen. Results of shade effects for each tree were averaged over distance and weighted by occurrence within each of three distance classes: 28 percent at 10 to 20 ft, 68 percent at 20 to 40 ft, and 4 percent at 40 to 60 ft (McPherson and Simpson 1999). Results are reported for trees shading east-, south-, and west-facing surfaces. The conifer is included as a windbreak tree located greater than 50 feet from the residence so it does not shade the building. Our results for public trees are conservative in that we assumed that they do not provide shading benefits. For example, in Modesto, California, 15 percent of total annual dollar energy savings from street trees was due to shade and 85 percent due to climate effects (McPherson et al. 1999).

Calculating climate effects—
In addition to localized shade effects, which were assumed to accrue only to residential yard trees, lowered air temperatures and windspeeds from increased neighborhood tree cover (referred to as climate effects) produced a net decrease in demand for winter heating and summer cooling (reduced windspeeds by themselves may increase or decrease cooling demand, depending on the circumstances). Climate effects on energy use, air temperature, and windspeed, as a function of neighborhood canopy cover, were estimated from published values (McPherson and Simpson 1999). Existing tree canopy cover for Queens was 20 percent and building cover was estimated to be 15 percent based on Grove and colleagues (2006). Canopy cover was calculated to increase by 2.2, 4.5, 8.9, and 3.0 percent for 20-year-old, small, medium, and large deciduous and coniferous trees, respectively, based on an effective lot size (actual lot size plus a portion of adjacent street and other rights-of-way) of 10,000 ft^2, and one tree on average was assumed per lot. Climate effects were estimated by simulating effects of air-temperature and wind reductions on energy use. Climate effects accrued for both public and yard trees.

Calculating windbreak effects—
Trees near buildings result in additional windspeed reductions beyond those from the aggregate effects of trees throughout the neighborhood. This leads to a small

additional reduction in annual heating energy use of about 0.5 percent per tree for conifers in the Mid-Atlantic region (McPherson and Simpson 1999). Yard and public conifer trees were assumed to be windbreaks, and therefore located where they did not increase heating loads by obstructing winter sun. Windbreak effects were not attributed to deciduous trees because their crowns are leafless during winter and do not block winds near ground level.

Atmospheric Carbon Dioxide Reduction

Calculating reduction in carbon dioxide emissions from power plants—
Conserving energy in buildings can reduce carbon dioxide (CO_2) emissions from power plants. These avoided emissions were calculated as the product of energy savings for heating and cooling based on CO_2 **emission factors** (table 18) and were based on data for the Northeast region where the average fuel mix is 29.0 percent coal, 28.0 percent nuclear, 20.5 percent natural gas, 10.4 percent fuel oil, 8.8 percent hydro, and 3.2 percent biomass/other (US EPA 2003). Fuel mixes and emissions outputs for the region are based on a population-weighted average for the portions of the states that are included in the region. For each state, the percentage of people living within the region was estimated. Values for each component of the fuel mix and the emissions outputs for each component (US EPA 2003) were then multiplied by the percentage of affected residents for each state. Finally, the fractional amounts for the fuel mix components and the emissions outputs were summed for all states. The value of $0.003 per lb CO_2 reduction (table 18) was based on the average value in Pearce (2003).

Calculating carbon storage—
Sequestration, the net rate of CO_2 storage in above- and belowground biomass over the course of one growing season, was calculated by using tree height and d.b.h. data with biomass equations (Pillsbury et al. 1998). Volume estimates were converted to green and dry-weight estimates (Markwardt 1930) and divided by 78 percent to incorporate root biomass. Dry-weight biomass was converted to carbon (50 percent) and these values were converted to CO_2. The amount of CO_2 sequestered each year is the annual increment of CO_2 stored as biomass each year.

Calculating CO_2 released by power equipment—
Tree-related emissions of CO_2, based on gasoline and diesel fuel consumption during tree care in our survey cities, were calculated by using the value 0.15 lb CO_2/in d.b.h. (Lu 2006). This amount may overestimate CO_2 release for less intensively maintained residential yard trees.

Calculating carbon dioxide released during decomposition—

To calculate CO_2 released through decomposition of dead woody biomass, we conservatively estimated that dead trees were removed and mulched in the year that death occurred, and that 80 percent of their stored carbon was released to the atmosphere as CO_2 in the same year (McPherson and Simpson 1999).

Calculating reduction in air pollutant emissions—

Reductions in building energy use also result in reduced emission of air pollutants from power plants and space-heating equipment. Volatile organic hydrocarbons (VOCs) and nitrogen dioxide (NO_2)—both precursors of ozone (O_3) formation—as well as sulfur dioxide (SO_2) and particulate matter of <10-micron diameter (PM_{10}) were considered. Changes in average annual emissions and their monetary values were calculated in the same way as for CO_2, by using utility-specific emissions factors for electricity and heating fuels (Ottinger et al. 1990, US EPA 1998). The price of emissions savings were derived from models that calculate the marginal damage cost of different pollutants to meet air quality standards (Wang and Santini 1995). Emissions concentrations were obtained from US EPA (2003; table 18), and population estimates from the U.S. Census Bureau (2006).

Calculating pollutant uptake by trees—

Trees also remove pollutants from the atmosphere. The modeling method we applied was developed by Scott et al. (1998). It calculates **hourly pollutant dry deposition** per tree expressed as the product of deposition velocity ($V_d = 1/[R_a + R_b + R_c]$), pollutant concentration (C), canopy-projection area (CP), and a time step, where R_a, R_b and R_c are aerodynamic, boundary layer, and stomatal resistances. Hourly deposition velocities for each pollutant were calculated during the growing season by using estimates for the resistances ($R_a + R_b + R_c$) for each hour throughout the year. Hourly concentrations for 2003 for NO_2, SO_2, O_3 and PM_{10} for New York City and the surrounding area were obtained from the US EPA. Hourly air temperature and windspeed data were obtained from the National Oceanic and Atmospheric Administration, and solar radiation data were calculated by using the Northeast Regional Climate Center's solar radiation model based on weather data from John F. Kennedy (JFK) airport (for a description of the model, see DeGaetano et al. 1993). The year 2003 was chosen because data were available and it closely approximated long-term, regional climate records. To set a value for pollutant uptake by trees we used the procedure described above for emissions reductions (table 18). The monetary value for NO_2 was used for ozone.

Estimating BVOC emissions from trees—

Annual emissions for biogenic volatile organic compounds (BVOCs) were estimated for the three tree species by using the algorithms of Guenther et al. (1991, 1993). Annual emissions were simulated during the growing season over 40 years. The emission of carbon as isoprene was expressed as a product of the base emission rate (micrograms of carbon per gram of dry foliar biomass per hour), adjusted for sunlight and temperature and the amount of dry, foliar biomass present in the tree. Monoterpene emissions were estimated by using a base emission rate adjusted for temperature. The base emission rates for the three species were based on values reported in the literature (Benjamin and Winer 1998). Hourly emissions were summed to get monthly and annual emissions.

Annual dry foliar biomass was derived from field data collected in New York City during the summer of 2005. The amount of foliar biomass present for each year of the simulated tree's life was unique for each species. Hourly air temperature and solar radiation data for 2003 described in the pollutant uptake section were used as model inputs.

Calculating net air quality benefits—

Net air quality benefits were calculated by subtracting the costs associated with BVOC emissions from benefits owing to pollutant uptake and avoided power plant emissions. A study in the Northeastern United States found that species mix had no detectable effects on O_3 concentrations (Nowak et al. 2000). The O_3-reduction benefit from lowering summertime air temperatures, thereby reducing hydrocarbon emissions from anthropogenic and biogenic sources, were estimated as a function of canopy cover following McPherson and Simpson (1999). They used peak summer air temperatures reductions of 0.2 °F for each percentage increase in canopy cover. Hourly changes in air temperature were calculated by reducing this peak air temperature at every hour based on hourly maximum and minimum temperatures for that day, scaled by magnitude of maximum total global solar radiation for each day relative to the maximum value for the year. However, this analysis does not incorporate the effects of lower summer air temperatures on O_3 formation rates owing to atmospheric processes.

Stormwater Benefits

Estimating rainfall interception by tree canopies—

A numerical simulation model was used to estimate annual rainfall interception (Xiao et al. 2000). The interception model accounted for water intercepted by the tree, as well as throughfall and **stem flow**. Intercepted water is stored temporarily on canopy leaf and bark surfaces. Rainwater drips from leaf surfaces, flows down the stem surface to the ground, or evaporates. Tree-canopy parameters that affect interception include species, leaf and stem surface areas, **shade coefficients** (visual density of the crown), foliation periods, and tree dimensions (e.g., tree height, crown height, crown diameter, and d.b.h.). Tree-height data were used to estimate windspeed at different heights above the ground and resulting rates of evaporation.

The volume of water stored in the tree crown was calculated from crown-projection area (area under tree dripline), **leaf area indices** (LAI, the ratio of leaf surface area to crown projection area), and the depth of water captured by the canopy surface. Gap fractions, foliation periods, and tree surface saturation storage capacity influence the amount of projected throughfall. Tree surface saturation was 0.04 in for all trees. Hourly meteorological and rainfall data for 2000 from the JFK airport (Station: JFK International Airport, New York City, NY; latitude 40°38'28.5" N, longitude 73°46'41.9" W) were used for this simulation. Annual precipitation during 2000 was 41.0 in. Storm events less than 0.1 in were assumed not to produce runoff and were dropped from the analysis. More complete descriptions of the interception model can be found in Xiao et al. (1998, 2000).

Calculating water quality protection and flood control benefit—
Treatment of runoff is one way of complying with federal Clean Water Act regulations by preventing contaminated stormwater from entering local waterways. Lacking data for Queens, we relied on stormwater management fees for Washington, D.C., as the basis for calculating the implied value of each gallon of stormwater intercepted by trees. In Washington, D.C., the monetized benefit value is $0.04/gal based on projected costs and water savings from the Water and Sewer Authority's 2002 Long-Term Control Plan (Greeley and Hansen 2002).

Aesthetic and Other Benefits

Many benefits attributed to urban trees are difficult to translate into economic terms. Beautification, privacy, wildlife habitat, shade that increases human comfort, sense of place and well-being are services that are difficult to price. However, the value of some of these benefits may be captured in the property values of the land on which trees stand.

To estimate the value of these "other" benefits, we applied results of research that compared differences in sales prices of houses to statistically quantify the difference associated with trees. All else being equal, the difference in sales price reflects the willingness of buyers to pay for the net benefit associated with trees. This approach has the virtue of capturing in the sales price both the benefits and costs of trees as perceived by the buyers. Limitations to this approach include difficulty determining the value of individual trees on a property, the need to extrapolate results from studies done years ago in the East and South to the Midwest region, and the need to extrapolate results from front-yard trees on residential properties to trees in other locations (e.g., back yards, streets, parks, and nonresidential land).

Anderson and Cordell (1988) surveyed 844 single-family residences in Athens, Georgia, and found that each large front-yard tree was associated with a 0.88-percent increase in the average home sales price. This percentage of sales price was used as an indicator of the additional value a resident in the Midwest region would gain from selling a home with a large tree.

The sales price of residential properties differed widely by location within the region. By averaging the values for several cities, we calculated the average home price for Northeast communities as $291,000. Therefore, the value of a large tree that added 0.88 percent to the sales price of such a home was $2,566. To estimate annual benefits, the total added value was divided by the LSA of a 30-year-old zelkova ($2,566/4,256 ft^2) to yield the base value of LSA, $0.60/ft^2. This value was multiplied by the amount of LSA added to the tree during 1 year of growth.

Calculating the aesthetic value of a residential yard tree—
To calculate the base value for a large tree on private residential property we assumed that a 30-year-old zelkova in the front yard increased the property sales price by $2,566. Approximately 75 percent of all yard trees, however, are in backyards (Richards et al. 1984). Lacking specific research findings, it was assumed that backyard trees had 75 percent of the impact on "curb appeal" and sales price compared to front-yard trees. The average annual aesthetic benefit for a tree on private property was estimated as $0.45/ft^2 LSA. To estimate annual benefits, this value was multiplied by the amount of LSA added to the tree during 1 year of growth.

Calculating the base value of a public tree—
The base value of a public tree was calculated in the same way as front-yard trees. However, because street and park trees may be adjacent to land with little value or resale potential, an adjusted value was calculated. A citywide street tree reduction factor (91 percent) was applied to prorate trees' value based on the assumption that public trees adjacent to different land uses make different contributions to property sales prices. For this analysis, the land use factor reflects the proportion of street trees in Queens by land use and the reduction factor is the value of a tree in an area of that use relative to single-home residential. Land use and reduction factors, shown respectively, were single-home residential (76 percent, 100 percent), multi-home residential (10 percent, 70 percent), small commercial (8 percent, 66 percent),

industrial/institutional/large commercial (6 percent, 40 percent), park/vacant/other (2 percent, 40 percent) (Gonzales 2004, McPherson 2001)

Although the impact of parks on real estate values has been reported (Hammer et al. 1974, Schroeder 1982, Tyrvainen 1999), to our knowledge, the onsite and external benefits of park trees alone have not been isolated (More et al. 1988). After reviewing the literature and recognizing an absence of data, we made the conservative estimate that park trees have half (50 percent) as much impact on property prices as street trees.

Given these assumptions, typical large street and park trees we estimated to increase property values by $0.55 and $0.30/ft^2 LSA, respectively. Assuming that 80 percent of all municipal trees were on streets and 20 percent in parks, a weighted average benefit of $0.50/ft^2 LSA was calculated for each tree.

Calculating Costs

Tree management costs were estimated based on surveys of municipal foresters and commercial arborists in the region.

Planting–

Planting costs include the cost of the tree and the cost for planting, staking, and mulching the tree. Based on our survey of Northeast municipal and commercial arborists, planting costs depend on tree size. Costs ranged from $200 for a 1-in tree to $1,000 for a 3-in tree. In this analysis we assumed that a 2-in yard tree was planted at a cost of $600. The cost for planting a 2-in public tree was $400.

Pruning

Pruning costs for public trees–

After studying data from municipal forestry programs and their contractors, we assumed that young public trees were inspected and pruned once during the first 5 years after planting, at a cost of $15 per tree. After this training period, pruning occurred once every 10 years for all trees. Pruning costs were $35, $70, and $280 for small (<20 ft tall), medium (20 to 40 ft tall), and large trees (>40 ft tall). More expensive equipment and more time was required to prune large trees than small trees. After factoring in pruning frequency, annualized costs were $3, $3.50, $7, and $28 per tree for public young, small, medium, and large trees, respectively.

Pruning costs for yard trees–

Based on findings from our survey of commercial arborists in the Northeast region, pruning cycles for yard trees were more frequent than reported for public trees. We assumed that young yard trees were inspected and pruned almost annually during the first 5 years after planting, and once every 4 years thereafter. However, survey findings indicate that only 20 percent of all private trees are professionally pruned and the number of professionally pruned trees increases as the trees grow (Summit and McPherson 1998). Accordingly, we assumed that professionals are paid to prune all large trees, 60 percent of the medium trees, and only 6 percent of the small and young trees and conifers. Using these contract rates, along with average pruning prices ($150, $400, $600, and $800 for young, small, medium, and large trees, respectively), the average annual costs for pruning a yard tree were $1.50, $1.27, $17.28, and $38.40 for young, small, medium, and large trees, respectively.

Tree and Stump Removal

The costs for tree removal and disposal were $18.33/in d.b.h. for public trees, and $50/in d.b.h. for yard trees. Stump removal costs were $6.5/in d.b.h. for public and $10/in d.b.h. for yard trees. Therefore, total costs for removal and disposal of trees and stumps were $24.84/in d.b.h. for public trees, and $60/in d.b.h. for yard trees.

Pest and Disease Control

Expenditures for pest and disease control in the Northeast are modest. They averaged about $0.22 per tree per year or approximately $0.02/in d.b.h. for public trees. Results of our survey indicated that only a few yard trees were treated, so we assumed no expenditures for treating pests and diseases in yard trees.

Irrigation Costs

Rain falls fairly regularly throughout most of the Northeast region and sufficiently that irrigation is not usually needed after establishment. In New York City, trees are watered for the first two summers after planting. We included initial irrigation costs with planting costs in this report.

Other Costs for Public and Yard Trees

Other costs associated with the management of trees include expenditures for infrastructure repair/root pruning, leaf-litter cleanup, litigation/liability, and inspection/administration. Cost data were obtained from the municipal arborist survey and assume that 80 percent of public trees are street trees and 20 percent are park trees. Costs for park trees tend to be lower than for street trees because there are fewer conflicts with infrastructure such as power lines and sidewalks.

Infrastructure conflict costs—
Many Northeast municipalities have a substantial number of large, old trees and deteriorating sidewalks. As trees and sidewalks age, roots can cause damage to

sidewalks, curbs, paving, and sewer lines. Sidewalk repair is typically one of the largest expenses for public trees (McPherson and Peper 1995). Infrastructure-related expenditures for public trees in Northeast communities were comparable to other regions, averaging approximately $3.28 per tree on an annual basis. Roots from most trees in residential yards do not damage sidewalks and sewers. Therefore, we did not include this cost for yard trees.

Liability costs—

Urban trees can incur costly payments and legal fees owing to trip-and-fall claims. A survey of Western U.S. cities showed that an average of 8.8 percent of total tree-related expenditures was spent on tree-related liability (McPherson 2000). However, communities in our Northeast survey did not report any tree-related liability expenditures. Therefore, we did not include costs for public or yard trees.

Litter and storm cleanup costs—

The average annual per-tree cost for litter cleanup (i.e., street sweeping, storm-damage cleanup) was $0.74/tree ($0.05/in d.b.h.). This value was based on average annual litter cleanup costs and storm cleanup, assuming a large storm results in extraordinary costs about once a decade. Because most residential yard trees are not littering the streets with leaves, it was assumed that cleanup costs for yard trees were 10 percent of those for public trees.

Green-waste disposal costs—

Green-waste disposal and recycling costs were considerable for our survey of Northeast communities, where 75 to 95 percent of green waste is recycled as mulch, compost, firewood, or other products. Fees from the sale of these products partially offset the costs of processing and hauling. However, tipping fees for disposal of green waste in landfills are relatively high. Survey results indicate that the average annual per-tree cost for green-waste disposal is $3.23 per public tree ($0.27/in d.b.h.). We assumed that disposal costs for yard trees were 10 percent of those for public trees, and this cost is shown under the category Administration/Inspection/Other. Tree removal and green-waste disposal costs associated with losses from exotic forest pests like Asian long-horned beetle and Emerald ash borer can be substantial, and are not included in any part of this analysis.

Inspection and administration costs—

Municipal tree programs have administrative costs for salaries of supervisors and clerical staff, operating costs, and overhead. Our survey found that the average annual cost for inspection and administration associated with street- and park-tree management was $5.96 per tree ($0.50/in d.b.h.). Trees on private property do not accrue this expense.

Calculating Net Benefits

When calculating net benefits, it is important to recognize that trees produce benefits that accrue both on- and offsite. Benefits are realized at four scales: parcel, neighborhood, community, and global. For example, property owners with onsite trees not only benefit from increased property values, but they may also directly benefit from improved human health (e.g., reduced exposure to cancer-causing UV radiation) and greater psychological well-being through visual and direct contact with plants. However, on the cost side, increased health care may be incurred because of nearby trees owing to allergies and respiratory ailments related to pollen. We assumed that these intangible benefits and costs were reflected in what we term "aesthetics and other benefits."

The property owner can obtain additional economic benefits from onsite trees depending on their location and condition. For example, carefully located onsite trees can provide air-conditioning savings by shading windows and walls and cooling building microclimates. This benefit can extend to adjacent neighbors who benefit from shade and air-temperature reductions that lower their cooling costs.

Neighborhood attractiveness and property values can be influenced by the extent of tree canopy cover on individual properties. At the community scale, benefits are realized through cleaner air and water, as well as social, educational, and employment and job training benefits that can reduce costs for health care, welfare, crime prevention, and other social service programs.

Reductions in atmospheric CO_2 concentrations owing to trees are an example of benefits that are realized at the global scale.

Annual benefits (B) are calculated as:

$B = E + AQ + CO_2 + H + A$ where

E = value of net annual energy savings (cooling and heating)

AQ = value of annual air-quality improvement (pollutant uptake, avoided power plant emissions, and BVOC emissions)

CO_2 = value of annual CO_2 reductions (sequestration, avoided emissions, release owing to tree care and decomposition)

H = value of annual stormwater-runoff reductions

A = value of annual aesthetics and other benefits

On the other side of the benefit-cost equation are costs for tree planting and management. Expenditures are borne by property owners (irrigation, pruning, and removal) and the community (pollen and other health care costs). Annual costs (C) equal the costs for residential yard trees (C_Y) and public trees (C_P):

$$C_Y = P + T + R + D + I + S + Cl + L$$

$$C_P = P + T + R + D + I + S + Cl + L + A \quad \text{where}$$

P = cost of tree and planting

T = average annual tree pruning cost

R = annualized tree and stump removal and disposal cost

D = average annual pest- and disease-control cost

I = annual irrigation cost

S = average annual cost to repair/mitigate infrastructure damage

Cl = annual litter and storm cleanup cost

L = average annual cost for litigation and settlements of tree-related claims

A = annual program administration, inspection, and other costs

Net benefits are calculated as the difference between total benefits and costs:

Net benefits = $B - C$